Planning a
Small Garden

First published 1998 in Great Britain by Hamlyn, an imprint of Octopus
Publishing Group Limited. North American edition published 1998
by SOMA Books, by arrangement with Hamlyn.

SOMA Books is an imprint of Bay Books & Tapes, Inc.,
555 De Haro St., No. 220, San Francisco, CA 94107.

For the Hamlyn edition:
Publishing Director: Laura Bamford
Creative Director: Keith Martin
Executive Editor: Julian Brown
Editor: Karen O'Grady
Senior Designer: Geoff Fennell
Design: Steve Byrne
Production Controller: Julie Hadingham
Picture Research: Zoe Holterman

For the SOMA edition:
Publisher: James Connolly
Art Director: Jeffrey O'Rourke
Editorial Director: Clancy Drake
Production: Ken Rackow
North American Editor: Suzanne Sherman
Proofreader: Marianna Cherry

Library of Congress Cataloging-in-Publication
Data on file with the Publisher

ISBN 1-57959-035-7

Printed in China
10 9 8 7 6 5 4 3 2 1

Distributed by Publishers Group West

Planning a
Small Garden

Richard Bird

SOMA
san francisco

contents

introduction

In the garden, you can work as hard as you want. Many people want big results from a small amount of effort, while others find that it is the effort as much as the results that they enjoy and so are prepared to work. Like many skills, some are born to gardening while others have to work hard at it. However, with a little common sense and a little honest effort, anyone can grow plants successfully. And with a little thoughtful planning, anyone should be able to create a garden to suit themselves and their family without spending a fortune. The trick is knowing what you want, which is where this book comes in: It will help you decide.

The worksheet that appears at the front of this book has been designed to help with the initial planning stages. Issues related to the physical aspects of the garden are considered, along with practical concerns such as time and effort, and lifestyle factors including the needs of children and the elderly. Your responses to the worksheet will lead directly to relevant sections of the book where preliminary ideas are discussed and expanded upon. Each section contains cross-references that will lead to even more possibilities.

When space is limited it becomes increasingly necessary to consider what is required of the garden. Practical concerns, such as the needs of children, can often outweigh aesthetic ones, like the desire for an immaculate lawn. Creating a small garden that satisfies your needs on both aesthetic and functional levels demands forethought and vision. That said, it is surprising what can be done with even the smallest patch of land. Visiting other gardens and looking at books will help generate new ideas to complement your own inventiveness. An emphasis should always be placed on your personal expression: Your garden should ultimately be a reflection of your personality.

When you first begin planning your garden, it is an excellent idea to sit down and make a list of what you need from the garden. The requirements should then be ranked in order of priority, as there might not be room for them all, or as some uses might conflict with others. For example, leaving space for children to play is likely to conflict with efforts at keeping an ordered, uncluttered garden, or the best-manicured lawn in the neighborhood. There is space on the worksheet in the front of this book to write down your prioritized list. Ideally, good planning can allow a garden to blend formal and more casual styles or elements, or to contain each in separate areas.

Your gardening needs and interests can also change over time. A garden is not a static object; it can be changed from time to time in much the same manner as house decoration—although plants do take a little longer to settle in than paint does to dry. If you plan your garden with the future in mind, that space you allocated for children's games may be transformed into a dream lawn once the children have grown.

It is also a good idea to draw a garden plan, marking in fixed features such as trees and sheds that you would like to retain. Also include areas of permanent shade and maximum sun, and any other relevant details. Then see if you can fit into that space the items from your list of requirements. (It is at this point that your prioritization will be important, as you may find that you don't have room to do everything you want, and will have to leave some things out.) You may wish to use the planning grid that appears on this book's worksheet.

When you have finished with your plan, go out into your garden and try to see whether it agrees with the space you have to work with. Mark out

areas with string along the ground to see how the space can be divided. Be patient. Do not begin digging right away: Give yourself a few weeks to live with the ideas and the plan you have made; look at the garden in different kinds of light and weather to see how it will all work. Make changes to your

Making use of space
The perfect small garden (opposite) with plenty of hard space on which to relax as well as lots of flowering plants in beds, containers and on the walls. All the space is used to the best advantage, and the result is an inviting garden, ideal for relaxing and entertaining friends.

plan as your instincts tell you. Use this opportunity to consider whether you will realistically have the time and money to do everything you want. Be aware that it is possible to take on more than you can manage and end up with a half-finished garden that becomes more of a burden than a

pleasure. When you are satisfied, it is time to start getting your hands dirty.

Gardening can be very rewarding. It allows you to create a peaceful space that is truly yours. It provides good, regular exercise and the opportunity to spend time in the open air. For many people, growing and propagating

plants is a fascinating and enduring pastime. And here lies one of gardening's severest problems: It can become addictive—you have been warned!

Evaluating the site

Be prepared

To get the most out of a garden it is essential that you study its physical aspects closely before beginning your work. One is usually in a hurry to get on and design the garden, but a period of assessment will ultimately save a lot of time and energy.

Soil conditions

The acidity of the soil may not be too much of a worry if there are no specific plant requirements; it is just a matter of making certain that the plants you buy will grow on your particular type of soil—most will. But there is a serious problem if you want to grow acid-loving plants, such as rhododendrons, and your soil is alkaline. There is little you can do about this except plant any such plants in compost in containers. A soil-testing kit can be bought very cheaply from garden centers and will provide a quick analysis of the soil. Most provide a checklist of what is required to redress any deficiencies found.

Too much water

Look for areas where water could pool when watering plants or after a rain. Waterlogged soil is hopeless for any sort of garden except for growing bog-loving plants. If the soil is soggy, especially if it has puddles on it, it should be drained. It may be possible to drain the water into a feature such as a pond. The alternative is to dig a soak-away (a large hole loosely filled with rubble) and lay land drains to carry the water from the soil into it.

Choosing the best beds

Some parts of the garden may have been used for beds before and may be in better condition than the rest of the garden. These will usually show up as being darker, freer draining, with soil that is easier to dig. It may be sensible to use these areas again if it fits in with the rest of the garden plan.

Sun and shade

Sun and shade are important to consider. Look carefully to discern where the shadows fall and where the best areas of sunlight are. Sunny areas may be used for patios or sitting areas where it would be pleasant to sit in the sun. Flower borders for sun-loving plants should be planted in these areas. Shady areas can be used for shade-loving plants as well as areas for sitting during very hot weather. Shady areas are not generally useful, so these can be the best places to put garbage cans or sheds.

What to keep

There is usually something that can be kept in a makeover garden. Trees, in general, should be kept, unless there are overwhelming reasons for removing them. Shrubs, beds, and lawns may already exist, but do not compromise your plan because of them. Remove them if need be. It is easy to establish new beds, and new plants will quickly grow to replace whatever grew there before. Unattractive existing features such as sheds, garages, greenhouses, or oil tanks can be incorporated into the scheme, making the most of them, or consider removing them completely.

Drawing a plan

Before starting to consider what to do with the garden it is a good idea to draw up a plan of the existing garden, showing every dimension and the position of all existing features and plantings. Be sure to include any unattractive features, such as manhole covers and drains. Once this has been done, when you sit around the kitchen table discussing or thinking about the new garden, you will be able to accurately see what you have, both in terms of the space there is to play with and the existing features that may be incorporated.

Time to look around

Finally, just walking around and looking at the garden from all angles, in all lights, and, if possible, in all seasons, will often suggest the ideal layout for the garden. Certain features will fit perfectly into certain places and the rest will slip into place around them. The garden will simply begin to take shape in your mind and then all you have to do is to make it happen!

Before you start
- Draw up a list of priorities
- Check soil conditions·
- Check sunny and shady areas
- Check access points
- Draw up plan of existing features
- Carry out basic tasks such as checking drainage, installing services, repairing or making fences

▶ ▶ Also see: Organic gardening, pages 46–47; Tool guide, pages 122–123

WORK

planning a

SHEET

small garden

W O R

These questions
are designed to help
you assess your
lifestyle needs,
practical concerns and
environmental factors.

Before creating the
small garden of your
dreams it is essential
to plan carefully.

Use each section
to discover how to
create the ideal small
garden for you.

E   E   T

Draw a map of your garden space here

K   S   H

How do you want the garden to be, or feel?

☐   Romantic   *24–29*

☐   Exotic   *54–59*

☐   Organic/natural   *42–46*

☐   Private   *116–120*

What kinds of special features

do you want to consider?

☐   Swimming pool   *22–23*

☐   Summerhouse   *24–25*

☐   Greenhouse   *56–57*

☐   Trellises/arches/pergolas   *66–67, 92–93*

☐   Terraces   *104–105*

☐   Tree house   *34–35*

☐   Fountain or pond   *48–53*

What existing limitations must you

consider?

☐   Driveway   *90–91*

☐   Slope   *102–107*

☐   Utility areas   *112–115*

Make a list of your gardening priorities here

_____

_____

_____

_____

_____

_____

_____

_____

_____

_____

_____

_____

_____

_____

_____

_____

_____

_____

_____

_____

_____

low maintenance

Less is more.

It is possible to get carried away when designing a garden, forgetting just how much work is involved in its maintenance. There is no doubt that the best gardens do need a lot of attention, more than most people can afford to give them, but with careful planning, a very attractive garden that only requires the minimum of effort can be created.

How much time do you have?

Before deciding which type of garden to create it is important to decide how much time can be spent on it and how this time is broken down. If time is limited to a couple of hours on weekends then it is important to design a low-maintenance garden, especially as some weekends will be lost through bad weather. If you can spare an hour a day, then the possibilities are much greater and there can be a greater emphasis on time-consuming flowering borders.

To mow or not to mow

One of the great time consumers is mowing the lawn. What is the lawn used for? Is it possible to use an alternative? A hard surface, such as paving or brickwork, needs little attention apart from occasional sweeping. Tanbark is a much softer surface, softer even than grass, and it makes a good alternative for play areas.

Hard boundaries

Similarly, hedges will need to be cut, so use solid fences as a boundary instead. If hedges are preferred, use a slow-growing one such as yew, which takes longer to establish but once grown needs only one trim a year.

Who wants to weed?

While some gardeners actually like weeding, to the majority it is not only a great waste of time, but also extremely tedious. Cut this out and a great deal of time is saved. Weedkillers are one alternative but apart from the initial clearing of the ground they are not recommended in an established garden for a wide variety of reasons including safety. The way to combat weeds is to use a mulch. Cover the borders with 10cm (4in) of bark and weed seed will not germinate.

Who wants to water?

Another boring and time-consuming job is watering lawns and plants. If you have to water, it is possible to use mechanical devices such as sprinklers, but it is much better to reduce the amount of water required by mulching. The mulch prevents the water from evaporating from the surface of the soil, leaving it in the ground and available to the plants.

Are there plants to save time?

The choice of plants is important if you want to save time, as some plants require more attention than others. For example, a fair number of shrubs and most small trees require little, if any, pruning. When buying, check just how much attention each requires. The same is true of many perennials—some need to be staked, deadheaded, and divided at regular intervals, while others seem to thrive on inattention. Again, check when buying.

Small is beautiful.

Reduce the amount of garden you have to look after by growing in pots and other containers. Containers require more watering than the open borders but overall they require less attention and can produce very satisfying results with relatively little effort.

Low-maintenance surfaces
Paved areas are much easier to maintain than grassy ones. In a small garden, their clear lines and uncluttered surface makes the space seem larger. As well as presenting far less work than a lawn, paving also cuts the cost and storage requirements for machinery and tools to maintain it.

container planting

Using containers is an ideal way of looking after plants in a small garden. It allows much greater flexibility than a conventional border, as groupings can be changed regularly. Plants can be kept out of sight until they are in flower, while dead ones can be removed. A wide range of plants—colorful annuals or leafy perennials—can be used, depending on the mood and effect required.

All in miniature
Containers can be used to brighten up areas of a garden or to provide different elements of the garden in miniature. Here, modern stainless steel pots contain lush grasses, echoing the lawns of larger gardens.

What to use
Containers can be anything from flowerpots to urns on pedestals, window boxes, or hanging baskets. There is a wide selection, each in a number of materials, available from garden centers. With ingenuity they can be recycled for other uses. Old, galvanized buckets and watering cans make splendid containers.

Planting
If the container is large or heavy, place it in its final position before filling it as it will be very heavy once filled with compost. Place a few small stones in the bottom of the container to help with drainage and then fill with a good compost. Plant the plants at the same depth as they were in their original containers. Water thoroughly.

Maintenance
It is essential to water containers regularly—at least once a day—in hot, dry weather. Feed once a week with a liquid feed added to the water during the summer months. The frequency of watering can be reduced by adding water-retaining granules to the compost at the time of planting. Similarly, a slow-release fertilizer added to the compost will supply nutrients for several months. Both are readily available in garden centers. Move tender and exotic plants under cover for the winter.

Types of Containers

	Advantages	Disadvantages
Terra-cotta	Attractive and relatively lightweight; difficult to overwater.	May be damaged by frost; loses moisture fast; may be expensive.
Stone	Attractive.	Heavy; expensive.
Cement	May be attractive; relatively cheap.	May look ugly; heavy.
Wood	May be attractive; relatively light; can be homemade.	Can rot; needs treating with preservative or paint.
Plastic	Inexpensive; lightweight.	Often very plain; easy to overwater.
Glass-fiber	Attractive reproductions.	Expensive.
Lead	Very attractive.	Very expensive; very heavy.

Recommended annuals and tender perennials
Ageratum
Alonsoa
Antirrhinum majus
Arcttotis stoechadifolia
Argyranthemum
Bidens ferulifolia
Brachycome iberidifolia
Convolvulus tricolor
Gazania
Helichrysum petiolare
Impatiens
Lobelia erinus
Osteospermum
Pelargonium
Petunia
Plectranthus coleoides
Semperflorens begonias
Senecio cineraria
Tagetes
Tropaeolum
Verbena hybrida
Viola wittrockiana

Recommended shrubs
Acer palmatum 'Dissectum'
Ballota pseudodictamnus
Buxus sempervirens
Callistemon citrinus
Camellia
Convolvulus cneorum
Cordyline australis
Erica
Fuchsia
Hebe
Helianthemum
Hydrangea
Hypericum
Ilex
Indigofera
Kalmia
Laurus nobilis
Lavandula
Olearia
Phormium
Pittosporum
Rhododendron
Rosmarinus
Skimmia
Yucca

Recommended perennials
Acanthus mollis
Agapanthus
Begonia x tuberhybrida
Dianthus
Diascia
Euphorbia
Hosta
Phormium
Primula
Sedum
Stachys byzantina

 ▶ ▶ Also see: Flower power, pages 68–69; Under glass, pages 56–57

Variety

Above: The scope for the use of containers in a small garden is tremendous, both in the shape and nature of the containers and in their contents. Be prepared to use unconventional containers or to use conventional containers in unconventional ways. Ingenuity is the key to success.

A fresh face

Left: One advantage of containers is that it is very easy to change the scene simply by rearranging the pots within their group. Alternatively, the pots can be regrouped in other parts of the garden. A third possibility is to introduce new containers into a grouping as their flowers come into bloom.

general low maintenance

Weeds in paving
If paving slabs are laid in the conventional way on sand without cement joints, weeds will grow between them. Laying down a sheet of black polyethylene first will keep weeds from coming up in the underlying soil. Cementing the joints between slabs will also prevent this, as well as preventing fresh weed seed from slipping in between the slabs.

In addition to choosing a garden design and plants that are low maintenance, there are also techniques that help to keep the amount of work to a minimum.

The key to success
There are two important things to remember in order to keep the work-load down—thorough preparation, and regular care.

Thorough preparation
Good preparation means there is less that is likely to go wrong in a garden. Make certain, for example, that all perennial weeds have been removed before any planting takes place as they will be at least twice as difficult to remove once plants are growing. Plenty of compost added to the soil when the beds are prepared will not only help to condition the soil, but it will also supply nutrients and help hold moisture down near the plant's roots, reducing the amount of feeding and watering required over several seasons.

Regular care
If a garden is not tended regularly, it can get out of hand. If weeds are pulled out when they are first seen, they are easy to control, but if they are allowed to grow freely, they intermingle with the plants and are very difficult to remove. A relaxing stroll round the garden every evening, removing any weed that has dared emerge during the day, will save many hours of work on a weekend, when there are likely to be many more important things to do. Similarly, catching pests at an early stage in their development will not only save time later on, but will also give the plants a better chance of survival in top condition.

Mulches
Use mulches to reduce the amount of watering and to prevent weeds from germinating. However, before laying down a mulch, remove any perennial weeds; a mulch will not prevent these from reappearing. Water the ground thoroughly before applying the mulch. Add mulch when it begins to thin.

Ground cover
Ground cover plants will also help reduce the amount of weeding required, but they will not prevent perennial weeds that are already in the soil from growing. Remove all visible weeds before planting a ground cover.

Staking
Staking perennial plants takes time. Choose plants that do not flop over at the first breath of wind. For plants at risk, stake them early, before they are half grown, as this is much easier than waiting until they are either fully grown or have already fallen over.

Mulches		
	Advantages	*Disadvantages*
Tanbark	Looks natural in most positions	Some of the bigger chips can be unattractive
Black polyethylene	Cheap, very efficient	Unattractive
Leaf-mold	Very natural, excellent soil conditioner	Not readily available unless homemade
Gravel	Attractive	Not suitable for all borders, becomes mixed into the earth and needs constant renewing
Spent mushroom compost	Excellent soil conditioner	Not good near acid-loving plants as it contains chalk
Farmyard manure	Excellent soil conditioner	Must not be used fresh, may contain weed seed
Grass cuttings	Readily available, best used at back of borders	Unattractive, must not be used in too deep a layer

▶ ▶ Also see: Quick tricks, pages 60–61; Container planting, pages 12–13

Living mulch
While plants must be given enough space to thrive, planting them as close together as possible reduces the amount of weeds that will grow in a bed or border. In effect, the plants create a living mulch or ground cover.

Evening stroll
Plants are kept in much better condition and are much easier to care for if they are attended to regularly. A five-minute relaxing stroll around the garden every evening will save hours of intensive work at a later stage.

Ground cover plants

Aegopodium
Asarum
Asperula
Aucuba
Brunnera
Carex
Claytonia
Convallaria
Cornus canadensis
Dryopteris
Epimedium
Euonymus fortunei
Euonymus japonica
Euphorbia amygdaloides robbiae
Gaultheria
Hedera
Hosta
Lamium
Lysimachia nummularia
Maianthemum
Pachysandra
Pulmonaria
Rhododendron
Sarcococca
Tiarella
Vaccinium
Vancouveria
Vinca

15

entertaining

Making the most of sunny days and warm evenings
One of the most delightful ways to use outside space is to share it with others. Entertaining guests during a warm summer evening or for a sunny lunch is one of the great joys in life. To do it in a relaxing, attractive atmosphere that you have created yourself increases the pleasure.

Location
When planning your garden with the thought of entertaining guests for cocktails and for sit-down meals, choose a site close to the house, and preferably a location that is easily accessible to the kitchen. However, if the area immediately next to the house is in constant shade, it may be better to locate the site where there is some sun, or at least dappled shade. Avoid windy positions, especially those where gaps between buildings cause vortices of wind even on still days. Be sure that garbage cans are out of sight and far enough away they cannot be smelled.

Enough space
The size of the area may depend on the space you have in the garden, but if possible, it ought to be tailored to your lifestyle. For dinners a deux, a small arbor can present the right kind of atmosphere. But most people will want to have space for a table that seats at least four, which will involve an absolute minimum area of 6 feet and seven inches. A larger area can be reduced to a more intimate setting by adding or moving containers of plants.

Shade
Shade is an important aspect to consider when selecting a site for entertaining. Some people like to entertain in full sun, but most prefer to eat in shade. Shade can be provided as a permanent feature or a temporary one by adding one or more patio umbrellas. A more elaborate structure that provides shade is an awning erected on poles or pulled out from a more permanent fixture on a wall. The design of these can be in subdued oatmeal color or vibrant stripes or multicolors.

A more rural atmosphere can be provided by creating shade with plants. This can be achieved with a tree or large shrub, or from climbers draped over a framework. Grapevines are extremely good in this respect as they supply a wonderful dappled shade that is ideal for protecting tables.

Barbecue
Depending on the type and scale of the entertaining, it may be desirable to include a barbecue in the area. This can be a permanent, built-in feature, or a mobile barbecue stored elsewhere (see page 18). Evening entertaining is likely to go on beyond nightfall, and some kind of lighting may be required. While candles create a romantic atmosphere, electric lighting may also be useful, so it is worth considering laying a permanent power line to service the area.

Plants
Planting an entertaining area leaves much room for choice. Fragrant climbers and other plants help create a relaxing atmosphere, while foliage plants help create a cool, restful ambience and add a sense of privacy. Flowers add a touch of gaiety or romance, depending on their colors. When selecting flowering plants keep in mind that whites and blues show up best in evening light.

Breakfast al fresco
Being able to dine outside whenever the weather permits is one of the great advantages of developing your own garden. Plants create the ideal surroundings for al fresco eating, whether it is a quick meal after work or a more relaxed dinner party. The constantly changing vegetation and flowers makes the backdrop more varied and interesting than an indoor room, and sweet summer air cannot be reproduced indoors.

barbecues

With portable barbecues and a wide range of cooking materials so readily available and easy to use, barbecuing has become a popular way of entertaining family and friends.

Permanent or portable?

There are three types of barbecues. A built-in barbecue which is a permanent structure; a portable one that can be moved around the garden; and a hybrid of the two, one made from bricks or concrete blocks that are dry-jointed and can be dismantled and rebuilt elsewhere should the mood take. Built-in barbecues can be part of the structure of one area of the garden, with low walls or built-in benches, a table, and storage facilities. A chimney helps to funnel away smoke and smells.

Where do you place it?

Siting should be carefully considered. Make certain there is enough room for all the guests. Barbecues generally take up more room than a more sedentary meal as there are frequently more guests and they often move about rather than sit around a table.

While it is convenient to be close to the house and the kitchen, cooking smells and smoke may annoy neighbors, so it is usually best to locate it as far away from the house as possible. Mobile barbecues are handy because you can move them to a position where smoke and smells do not affect your guests or neighbors. Avoid siting the barbecue too near plants, fences, or buildings that may scorch or even catch fire. Keep a fire blanket and water nearby, just in case there is a problem.

If possible, put the barbecue on a hard surface—a patio or stand; a hard surface is easier to clean and will take the trampling better than grass, especially if there has been recent rain.

Brick built-ins
Opposite: A built-in barbecue can be a simple structure, as pictured here, or it can be part of a larger complex that includes built-in benches, a table, and storage facilities. Leave plenty of room to maneuver around the barbecue and serve the food away from the cooking area.

Portables
Right: A portable barbecue does not fit into the garden as well aesthetically as a built-in one, but it is much more versatile. It can be moved to different areas, depending on the weather, and can be put out of sight when not in use. Small, tray-like portable barbecues can be used as the working parts inside a built-in structure. Although you can buy elaborate, expensive models, inexpensive basic portables are easily available and will do the job.

Fuels		
	Advantages	*Disadvantages*
Charcoal	Traditional barbecue fuel; easily available.	Need to wait at least 30 minutes for the right heat; can burn out.
Gas	Easy; clean; no waiting.	Not as much fun as creating your own fire.
Wood	Traditional campfire material; readily available.	Not easy to create enough heat with a small fire; smoke and soot taint the food.

   ▶▶ Also see: Disguising essentials, pages 112–113

Gas-fired grills
A modern gas-fired barbecue grill is one of the easiest and cleanest to operate. The only disadvantage is that a gas grill doesn't allow for some of the fun there can be in lighting one's own fire. Gas grills are powered by gas cylinders and are usually mobile, although they can be built-in. Gas grills should be stored under a cover.

Siting barbecues
- Mobile units allow you to position the barbecue according to conditions
- After other considerations, such as avoiding annoying your neighbors and guests with smoke and smells, place as near to kitchen as possible
- Avoid drafty positions
- Avoid scorching plants, fences, and buildings
- Allow plenty of space around the barbecue
- Place the barbecue on a hard surface

Building a barbecue
- Be sure it is well sited
- Make certain the structure is stable
- Allow enough grilling space
- Allow variable heights for grills
- Build up the wall above the grill to act as a windshield and build it high enough to avoid bending
- If possible, build the walls up to form a chimney to funnel smoke away
- Include space for tools, condiments, and cooked and uncooked food
- Plant herbs nearby—for easy access and pleasant aroma

Safety
- Make certain that the barbecue is stable
- Keep the barbecue away from flammable materials such as wooden fences by placing the barbecue at a safe distance from them
- Avoid damaging shrubs and other plants
- Keep children and pets under control
- Have a fire blanket and water on hand

furniture

Garden furniture should be chosen just as carefully as you choose furniture for the house. It should fit in with the overall appearance of the garden as well as having qualities such as comfort and ease of maintenance. If there are children around, it should be strong enough to take some abuse or be inexpensive enough to be replaced. Furniture can be very expensive, so the financial aspects should be considered carefully.

Stylish seating
A simple wooden bench can be ideal for a small garden. It has a simple elegance about it as a decorative feature as well as a practical one, for sitting. If the bench is wood, regular maintenance will be required to keep it in good condition. If it is plastic, apart from an occasional wipe-down, no regular maintenance is required.

Comfort
Most types of seating benefits from the use of cushions. Cushions add comfort and they also add color. Some are made with fabrics that allow them to be left outside during the summer, but most are best kept indoors when not in use. In many small gardens there is little space to move around, and seating or tables can be built in as part of the patio area.

Materials
The weight of garden furniture is important. Stone is so heavy it needs to be placed permanently, while aluminum can easily be moved around to follow sun or shade.

Always consider the amount of maintenance required when selecting garden furniture. Some furniture needs more care than others, especially if it is to be left outside permanently.

Cheap seats
A simple, inexpensive seat can be built by bolting a plank of wood across two brick pillars or supporting it on two sections of tree trunk.

Seating and shade
The most useful garden furniture is seating, consisting of benches or individual seats. The seats can be heavy if permanently positioned, but need to be lighter if used around tables. Folding furniture, such as director's chairs, is a great advantage in a small garden, but it does need to be stored away in bad weather. For sunbathing or relaxing a range of loungers, swinging seats, and hammocks are available. Swinging seats come with their own framework, but hammocks need secure fixing on trees or in walls. Sunshades and umbrellas are also important pieces of garden furniture.

Materials

	Advantages	Disadvantages
Wood	Usually looks good; can be folding; can be painted; can be custom or home-built.	Inexpensive, lower-quality pieces can become loose and unstable; needs maintaining; needs covering or storing in winter; some woods last longer than others.
Plastic	Inexpensive; little maintenance required; lightweight; usually comfortable; can be folding.	Limited color range; looks like plastic; needs covering or storing in winter.
Steel and cast alloys	Solid, long-lasting; can be good-looking; can be painted.	Cold and hard without cushions; can rust if not maintained.
Aluminum	Inexpensive; little maintenance required; lightweight; can be folding.	Frequently looks cheap; fabric seats and backs not long-lasting; can become unstable; needs storing when not in use
Stone or faux stone	Heavy; looks permanent; usually blends in well; easy to maintain.	Cold; hard; cannot be moved; may need solid foundation.
Fabric	Wide range of colors; lightweight.	Needs to be stored when not in use.

▶ ▶ Also see: Illuminating the garden, pages 28–29; Barbecues, pages 18–19

Dining Out
Above: A small
space is all you need
for a table and a
couple of chairs and
you have the setting
for breakfast, lunch,
an evening meal, or
just a cup of coffee.
There's nothing like
dining or relaxing in
the fresh air.

Sunny Days
Left: This slatted
wooden lounger is a
perfect way to relax.
It is relatively light
and can be easily
moved around,
although it will
need some
maintenance to
keep its appearance
fresh. Although it is
shaped, the wood
may be too hard for
prolonged lounging.
Add cushions,
and you're set for
relaxing enjoyment
of your garden.

Key Points

Appearance
Comfort
Cost
Maintenance

Storage
requirements

Strength
Weight

fun & games

So often gardens can become serious places, where the sole purpose seems to be to act as custodian to a collection of plants. However, nothing can be more satisfying on a sunny afternoon or a warm evening than having a relaxed, pleasurable time with a few friends. This may mean simply sitting around enjoying food and conversation, or it may include activities and games.

Nets and hoops

Some games require little more than a lawn and can be set up whenever they are needed. The quality of the grass surface is immaterial. A scratch game of badminton can be played over a temporary net on any rectangular lawn. Croquet is another game that requires little more than a lawn (a few bumps in the lawn shouldn't matter as it will be the same for everyone playing). The great thing about these two games is that the lawn can be quickly cleared and another, different game played.

Going through hoops
Croquet was once the province of the wealthy with large gardens and immaculate lawns. But increasingly, people with smaller gardens are enjoying the game, even if it does mean bending the rules a bit to suit the size and shape of the lawn.

Mazes

Some people like games that require more of a permanent set-up. Clock golf, for example, may require one or more holes in the lawn, but other games may be far more elaborate. Mazes, for example, have aesthetic appeal and are great fun. Two-dimensional mazes may be created on the ground simply by mowing the grass in a pattern, or by using different colored bricks. Three-dimensional mazes, made from hedges, are more difficult to fit into a small garden.

Swimming

Many people would love to own a swimming pool. It is possible to have one in a small garden, either a constructed one, sunk into the ground, or a less expensive above-the-ground pool. This type of pool comes in kit form and can be erected by the owner, but constructed, sunken pools are much more complicated and are best built by professionals. If there are children in the area, be sure to take the necessary precautions.

Relax or work out
There is plenty of scope in a small garden for games and sport of all sort. A patio can provide the ideal site for table tennis (top). Guests old and young can enjoy a decorative maze laid in stone or cut in grass (above). If finances allow it, even a swimming pool (left) can be constructed in all but the smallest of gardens.

romantic images

Hearts and flowers
Gardens can be a haven of peace and quiet. With a little thought and the correct choice of plants even the most barren of sites can be transformed into a romantic paradise, a place for amorous encounters, or simply a place to relax after a day's work.

The right atmosphere
The mood of a garden is important, and one of the most popular is that which appeals to the romantic senses. Plants are mainly responsible for creating this atmosphere but structures, including summerhouses and arbors all contribute. It is important to choose your method of lighting carefully as it can create the perfect mood for sitting or strolling in the evening.

Privacy
The romantic garden needs to be private. It is particularly important to install boundaries using trees, shrubs, hedges, or even fences to create an atmosphere of intimacy. The garden should ideally consist of winding paths and individual areas divided from one another by plants.

Color
The colors in a romantic garden are of great importance. Bright, hot colors are not for this garden, except in occasional splashes. Soft pastel colors with their misty quality paint a more ethereal picture.

Fragrance
Fragrance is another of the most desirable qualities in plants for a romantic garden. Plenty of scented flowers and foliage that fingers can run through gives a garden a quality all of its own. Strongly scented paths along the drive or by the gate give a place a strong identity when people arrive.

Bowers
There must be plenty of places to sit and soak up the atmosphere in a romantic garden. Seats should be placed in various locations, some tucked amid shrubs or in arbors that are surrounded by climbing flowering plants. Again, as many of the plants as possible should be fragrant. If possible, the bowers should be big enough to also accommodate a table so meals may be taken in them.

Fixtures and fittings
Permanent garden furniture should not be plain or makeshift; it should fit in with the style of the garden. Wrought-iron or cast-iron furniture in Victorian or Edwardian designs and stone furniture is perfect. Stone or reproduction-stone statuary also adds to the scene when placed in the right settings. Suggested locations include focal points at the end of a bend in a path or peering from behind foliage. Stone urns are also very effective.

Water
Water also adds its magical qualities to a romantic garden. Water is full of reflections and sounds, and it can often be heard even if not seen. A small pond can be charming. Areas around ponds are often damp, forming the perfect situation for the large-leaved plants that love these conditions. These areas of dense foliage bring a certain gothic quality to the mood of the scene.

Setting the scene
With surprisingly little effort it is easy to turn a garden into a romantic setting in which to entertain or relax. Whether it is for two or more (or even simply for personal relaxation and enjoyment), a few fragrant plants and the right illumination will transform a garden or patio for a warm summer's evening.

romantic planting

One of the keys to a romantic garden is good, imaginative planting. The smell of fragrant plants, their soft colors and the hum of contented bees as they go about their business all contribute to the atmosphere and help create a haven of tranquility.

Sweeping beds

There may well not be much room in a small garden for sweeping beds of flowers, but with a bit of ingenuity, a good attempt can be made. One trick is to curve the borders so that they disappear out of sight behind other features, giving the impression that they go on for much further than they actually do. Use a wide range of plants that come into flower from spring to autumn to provide continuity. Soft, pastel colors are the most romantic and also have the advantage of receding from the eye, making the beds look larger. A solid block of color such as a hedge behind the beds is best for setting off the color of the flowers. Incorporate as many buddleia (butterfly plants) as possible, as their lilac flowers, which bloom on the shrub in spring and summer, add beauty and atmosphere. The drone of bees is very atmospheric, so add plenty of flowering plants for them to enjoy. Use the sunny side of the garden for these beds.

Nature's scents
One of the most evocative aspects of any garden is scent. Everything from the fragrance of flowers and foliage to the fresh, sweet smell of mown grass and the musky smell of decaying leaves add to the atmosphere that lingers in the mind. Lavender, seen here lining a path, is one of the most evocative of all plant aromas.

Rambling climbers

Climbing roses or honeysuckle, particularly the scented varieties are captivating. They can be coiled around bowers or arbors in sitting areas, or can be trained up poles, trellises, along ropes, or up through trees.

Overgrown gardens

Overgrown gardens have a romantic quality. However, it is better to have a controlled overgrown garden than it is to simply let one get out of control. An uncontrolled garden will soon decay and become anything but romantic. Use plenty of foliage plants, such as hostas and ferns, as well as dense trees and shrubs in a shadier, damper part of the garden. Prune plants as needed to keep the growth abundant, but in check.

Planting for the evening

Summer evenings are a special time, a time when many people like to relax in their gardens. Many plants are at their most fragrant in the evening and should therefore be planted near sitting areas. White flowers show up more than any others as the light begins to fade and they should be planted where they have the maximum impact.

▶ ▶ Also see: Bedding plants, pages 70–71; Exotic plants, pages 58–59

Nature's beauty
What better setting can there be for a romantic tryst than that of a garden full of flowers? Even a small plot can contain at least a few flowers, in small beds, in containers, or growing up walls or fences. Some flowers are more romantic than others. In spring, camellias (left) must head the list, while roses more than hold their own in summer.

White flowers

Achillea ptarmica 'The Pearl'
Amelanchier
Anaphalis margaritacea
Anemone x hybrida 'Honorine Jobert'
Anthemis punctata cupaniana
Arabis
Argyranthemum frutescens
Aster novae-angliae 'Wedding Lace'
Astilbe 'Irrlicht'
Bellis perennis
Camellia 'Swan Lake'
Campanula persicifolia
Centranthus ruber 'Albus'
Cerastium tomentosum
Choisya ternata
Chrysanthemum
Clematis 'Marie Boisselot'
Convallaria majalis
Convolvulus cneorum
Crambe cordifolia
Dianthus
Digitalis purpurea 'Alba'
Epilobium angustifolium 'Album'
Erica
Eucryphia
Galanthus
Geranium
Gypsophila
Hebe salicifolia
Hydrangea
Iberis sempervirens
Iris
Jasminum
Lamium maculatum 'White Nancy'
Lathyrus
Leucanthemum
Lilium
Lychnis coronaria 'Alba'
Magnolia
Malva moschata 'Alba'
Myrrhis odorata
Nicotiana sylvestris
Olearia
Osmanthus
Osteospermum
Paeonia
Penstemon
Petunia
Philadelphus
Phlox
Physostegia virginiana 'Alba'
Polygonatum x hybridum
Prunus
Pulmonaria 'Sissinghurst White'
Rhododendron
Rosa
Smilacina
Spiraea 'Arguta'
Syringa vulgaris 'Mont Blanc'
Tulipa
Viola
Zantedeschia aethiopica

Fragrant flowers and foliage

Azara
Berberis x stenophylla
Choisya ternata
Chrysanthemum
Clethra
Convallaria majalis
Corylopsis
Crambe
Daphne
Dianthus
Elaeagnus
Erysimum
Galanthus
Hamamelis
Hesperis
Hyacinthus
Itea virginica
Laurus nobilis
Lavandula
Lonicera
Lupinus
Magnolia
Mahonia
Monarda
Myrtus
Oenothera
Osmanthus
Philadelphus
Phlox
Primula
Rhododendron luteum
Rosa
Rosmarinus officinalis
Santolina
Sarcococca
Skimmia
Viburnum
Viola

illuminating the garden

Good lighting
Carefully chosen lighting enhances the atmosphere of the garden. Glaring lighting, on the other hand, lacks the necessary subtlety and often flattens the garden's appearance. There is a very large range of lighting, both with naked flames and electricity, that can be used to flatter your garden and create the right atmosphere.

For many people, it is the evening when the garden is at its most relaxing, particularly after a day's work. Carefully chosen lighting can effectively enhance the mood. Of course, lighting is also essential for security and for finding one's way around.

Reasons for illuminating the garden include:
- Seeing your way around
- Security concerns
- The magical effect of lighting plants
- Localized lighting for eating or sitting

Blanket cover
The easiest lighting method is to have blanket cover from a lamp placed high on a building or post so that it completely illuminates the area below it. A much more subtle approach is to have a series of individual lamps wherever they are needed, along the path or drive, beside steps, and near sitting areas. There is a whole range of possibilities with lights on posts and other types of fittings to suit individual garden styles. Creating shadow is as important as lighting other areas, so only illuminate the areas that really need it.

Flood-lighting
The same principle applies to illuminating for effect. Do not light all the trees, shrubs, and other plants with a single, even spread. Use several lamps, and remember when placing them that shade effects are as important as the illuminated areas.

On/off
There is no need for lights to be on permanently. Time switches can be used with flood lighting. Motion-detector lights can be used to switch lights on and off on paths and drives. Using the lights only when they are needed not only saves electricity but also reduces light pollution.

Temporary lighting
It is possible to install temporary lighting for a particular event. This will usually involve having cables draped around, so special low-voltage lighting is recommended. Temporary lighting comes in many forms, including lanterns for hanging and pedestal units for sticking into the ground along paths or around the edge of a patio.

▶ ▶ Also see: Entertaining, pages 16–17

Real flames

Temporary garden illumination
need not be restricted to electric
lighting. Candles, flaming torches, and
kerosene lamps are much softer and
have a somewhat magical quality.
Flaming torches are particularly good
for parties.

Underwater illumination

Ponds and fountains can look
spectacular when lit, especially from
below the water. However, special
lighting is required, and it must be
safely installed.

Safety
- Only use lighting equipment designed
  specifically for the outdoors
- Use the correct cabling to power
  sources
- Have professionally installed equipment
- Check regularly for wear or problems
- Keep flames away from flammable
  material

young children

Young at heart

Like the rest of the house, a garden must reflect the needs and habits of those who use it. When couples with children contemplate designing their first garden, they need to take their kids into consideration. Pristine borders and manicured lawns will most likely have to wait until the children grow up. A garden that kids can use is the perfect playground. It can provide a secure environment where they can play safely in the fresh air. It allows them to develop all kinds of motor skills, from riding bicycles to climbing trees, all under the watchful eye of their parents, and it can leave them with an undying love of gardens and plants, something to enjoy for the rest of their lives.

Designing for children

Children will want to play ball, dig holes, and build camps, so it is best to accept this and design the garden accordingly. Large open spaces for football, trees for climbing, and shrubs for hiding are all part of the fun. Many children like to have things built for them, especially when they are very young. Sandboxes, treehouses, and supervised wading pools are always welcome.

No-go areas

As long as there is plenty of space for children to use, there is no need to turn the whole garden over to them. Leave room for flower borders and areas for adults to relax in comfort, but learn to live with the occasional ball breaking off flowers or the bicycle accidentally mowing down a shrub. Romantic gardens in particular remain in children's memories. For many adults, the fragrance and color of many plants are associated with childhood, so make the garden resemble a garden rather than a barren war-zone.

Involve them

While many basic things, such as swings and sandboxes, do not change, each generation has its own idea of fun, and parents, regretfully, are a long way from childhood. So, when you are designing and building things for the children, let them get involved rather than offering them a "perfect" play area that you would have liked some twenty or thirty years ago.

Young gardeners

As well as providing youngsters with somewhere to play safely, a well-designed and well-used garden will also instill in them a love of gardens. One way to intensify this is to help young children to create their own garden. Short attention spans and lack of interest in dull, routine tasks often means that the parent will have to do a lot of the work, but nonetheless getting the kids involved is worth doing. Just a small plot will do. Annual flowers and vegetables make the most interesting subjects as something is always happening in the cycle from germination to dying back. Shrubs, on the other hand, can be rather dull as nothing much happens throughout the year except some possible flowering. Some seed merchants provide seed especially packeted for the needs of children.

Fleeing the nest

Children are not children forever, so plan with the future in mind. For example, when designing a sandbox, do it in such a way that it may be converted into a pond later on. Site the lawns for playing where you can envision a future lawn with better-quality grass. Plant trees and shrubs so they will mature by the time you get your garden back.

House in the trees
Creating the right atmosphere in which a child's mind can roam and invent is important to a child's development. What better way than creating a tree house? Having their own secluded world away from parents will forever keep the garden in their memories. Once the children have left the nest, the adults can take it over for their own use.

safety and security

Sensible precautions
In their search for new experiences, children are often oblivious to danger. It is important to be sure that all gates are firmly latched or even locked. Dangers from within can include falling from play equipment onto hard surfaces. The blow can be softened by using loose bark under play equipment to break the fall.

Children's welfare and security are a parent's first priority. There are obvious dangers in a garden that should be eliminated both for the sake of the children and for their parents' peace of mind.

Keep them in

One of the most important aspects of child safety in the garden is to make sure that they stay there. A child wandering away from the house or onto a road is a potentially dangerous situation.

Make certain that the garden is surrounded by an adequate boundary of some sort and that all gates are firmly closed and locked with child-proof or out-of-reach latches. Also, check to make certain that a child cannot slip through the bars of a gate or fence. Make certain that visitors, letter carriers, or sanitation workers do not leave gates that are directly connected to the children's area open.

Hard surfaces

While children need hard surfaces for certain types of games, especially during the winter, it is a good idea to use soft surfaces in areas where they are likely to fall. For example, tanbark can be used to cushion accidental falls from climbing frames or swings.

Out of sight, out of mind

Although play areas for young children may not be the most beautiful of sights, place them where they can be seen. As children get older and become better able to care for themselves, they tend to prefer to have areas of the garden that are secret and away from adults.

Who wants a sweet?

The berries of many plants can look like sweets to children. But many plants are poisonous and should be avoided. Even the roots of some poisonous plants, such as Aconitum, may look like potatoes and be eaten during a child's game. Other plants, while not poisonous, can cause harm by stinging or because of sharp thorns or stickers. There are plenty of plants that are safe to use, so take care to avoid those that are not.

Avoid:

Aconitum	Laburnum
Arum	Ligustrum
Colchicum	Rhamnus
Daphne	Ruta
Datura	Solanum
Digitalis	Taxus
Euphorbia	Wisteria
Heracleum	

▶ ▶ Also see: Entrances and exits, pages 88–89; Outer boundaries, pages 118–119

Water

Water features in a garden must be considered carefully for child safety. It is important to remember that it is possible to drown in even a few inches of water. If you want to use water, use fountains or spouts whose water disappears between stones into an underground reservoir so that there is no standing water to cause problems. If there is already a pond, make certain that it is securely fenced off or covered over when there are children around.

Glass

Most gardens contain glass somewhere, such as in a greenhouse, a cold frame, or cloches. Although not particularly satisfactory from a horticultural point of view, glass can be replaced by plastic, which is much safer. Alternatively, any areas containing glass can be fenced off. Another real danger can come from children falling onto the unprotected tops of canes, sticks, or any other pointed object.

Potential dangers for young children

- open gates
- broken fences
- unprotected pooled water
- poisonous plants
- glass
- hidden parts of the garden
- canes and pointed objects

Pond life

One of the greatest dangers in a garden is water. Children are naturally fascinated and drawn to it. All ponds should be securely fenced off or strongly covered in some way.

activities

Swings and sand pits
Right: Swings and ropes are among the most fundamental of children's playthings. They are readily available in a variety of materials, or can be homemade. It is important to make certain that they are secure, as children are likely to test them to their limits. The sand pit (below) is another simple plaything that will give hours of pleasure.

Children will always invent their own games, but it is frequently up to adults to provide the right environment for this to happen. This usually means supplying just a few basic things and letting the children work out the details. Lawns for play, bushes for hiding, and trees for climbing are the basics, and can provide hours of fun.

Playtime
As well as just lounging around in gardens, there are plenty of activities that children like to undertake. Many children are best left to their own devices, especially when they get a bit older, but there are still many things that you can do that will be appreciated.

Lawns
One essential is a flat lawn. The lawn is likely to get hard wear, so it is no use planting fine grasses as play will soon produce bald patches. Use tough grasses that can tolerate running feet.

Sand pits
For very young children, sand is a fascinating material, and a sand pit can supply hours of fun. Site the pit in a position where it can be used for a pool or some other feature when the children grow up. It can be constructed of wood, but should be free from splinters. Special sand can be purchased that is suitable for play without staining clothes or containing sharp pieces.

Climbing apparatus
Climbing provides healthy exercise and helps kids develop self-assurance and motor skills. A store-bought or homemade climbing frame is a great addition to any yard where children play. It is essential that the equipment be safely constructed and secure in the ground. Swings are also an eternal source of pleasure. Covering the ground with a 4-inch layer of chipped bark will help soften falls.

A secret garden
Most children love to have secret hideaways in a garden. Even the smallest garden can have its secret spots tucked away somewhere. Thick bushes and screened off areas help to provide this.

Tree houses
Tree houses are as much fun for adults as they are for children. Safety is, of course, of paramount importance. Since tree houses may be seen from neighboring properties, you may need to get planning permission to erect one in some areas. For younger children playhouses on the ground are a great source of fun. Plastic ones can be bought, but there is more fun to be had out of a homemade one in wood, especially if the children help build it.

Hard-wearing grasses used singly or in mixtures:

Axonopus – for warmer climates
Eremochloa ophiuroides – for warmer climates
Lolium perenne – for cooler climates
Paspalum notatum – for warmer climates
Poa pratensis – for cooler climates

Adventure
Climbing frames are
not only great fun
for children, but they
also help develop
many of their motor
skills, balance not
being the least of
them.
All frames should
be very strongly
made and secure in
the ground. Timber
should not only be
strong but free from
splinters. Let the
children help design
and build it for some

year-round interest

Making the most of it

Most people use their gardens only during the summer months, but there is no reason why gardens should not be used throughout the year, not necessarily for sitting in, although even that is possible in some areas, but at least for providing color and interest. A walk around a garden covered in frost or snow can be a magical experience.

Plants for all seasons

With a bit of careful planning it is possible to provide color in the garden year-round. There is, obviously, not much color in the winter, but it is surprising how many plants do flower at that time of year, and many have the added bonus of being fragrant. Even if they do not flower, many trees and shrubs have colorful bark that shows up at this time of year as there are no leaves to mask it.

Structure

In summer, when everything is grown to its full height, the garden is very three-dimensional. The varying heights not only add interest to the picture but they also mask or allow glimpses of what lies beyond, adding an element of intrigue into the design. In winter, much dies back to ground level and the garden can become very flat, especially if the planting relies mainly on annuals and herbaceous perennials. A few evergreen shrubs, or even the naked stems of deciduous shrubs, make all the difference.

Keeping it beautiful

Do not neglect the garden throughout the summer and autumn. Remove any dead flowers and stems that are dying back, partly to keep the garden neat and tidy and partly so that the plants that are in flower show to their best advantage. This is particularly important during times when there is not too much in flower.

While it is good to remove dead and dying material during the summer months, as the main flowering seasons come to an end in autumn leave some of the dead stems and seed heads for winter decoration. The brown stems not only look attractive when there is nothing else around, but they also provide food by way of seeds and sheltering insects for many birds.

Self-contained

One way of ensuring color in the garden year-round is to use containers—tubs, window boxes, or hanging baskets—to grow plants and flowers when there is frost on the ground. Most of the annual and tender plants used in the summer have a very long season, and thrive all through the warmer parts of the year. After the frost, however, there are various hardy plants, such as winter pansies, that can be used to give the garden life all year round.

Surfaces

While lawns and grass paths are fine for dry weather, they are not much use during wet seasons. Hard surfaces are much more practical, especially for paths in constant use. Areas immediately outside the house are particularly prone to wear, and this makes an ideal place for a hard-surfaced patio. A series of stepping stones will ease the wear on grass when it is wet so do keep your lawn, just protect it. Another compromise is to use gravel, which is not as hard in appearance as stone slabs or bricks.

Winter sunshine
Winter is the most difficult time in the garden, although with some effort on the part of the gardener, even the smallest garden can produce flowers to brighten the dull months. Winter aconites (*Eranthis hyemalis*) are the harbingers of spring. Once their golden goblets open, it is a sign that the warmer weather is not too far away.

seasonal plants and shrubs

Heady days
There is little more evocative of the heady days of summer than flowers that once bloomed in meadows and fields. It is possible to recreate this in a border, as here, with a mixture of corn marigolds (*Chrysanthemum segetum*), poppies (*Papaver rhoeas*), chamomile (*Chamaemelum nobile*) and cornflowers (*Centaurea cyanus*).

There is nothing more satisfying than creating an interesting and colorful garden, particularly one that is appealing throughout the year. Skillful use of plants and shrubs with different seasons of flowering, and attractive foliage, can help to ensure this, making the garden a place of everchanging beauty.

Mix and match

Mix the plants in borders so that there is always something colorful going on. If winter plants are allocated to one area then that area will become dull for the rest of the year.

Spring bulbs

Spring bulbs always have a very fresh look which is appropriate to their blooming season. Most types flower early and then die back for the rest of the year. This makes them ideal for planting among shrubs and herbaceous plants which will grow up and cover the spaces where the bulbs have flowered.

Summer bloom

Summer is the season when the real action begins in a garden. There seems to be something in bloom all the time. There are literally thousands of plants from which to choose. Check the flowering times when you buy your summer plants or seeds so that you get an even spread in early, mid-, and late summer. Do not forget to include some flowers for cutting for the house.

 ▶ ▶ Also see: Romantic planting, pages 26–27; Exotica, pages 54–55

Autumn color

Acer
Amelanchier
Berberis
Betula
Carpinus betulus
Cornus
Cotinus
Cotoneaster
Crataegus
Euonymus
Liquidambar
Malus
Prunus
Rhus typhina
Sorbus
Stephanandra

Winter-flowering

Abeliophyllum distichum
Chimonanthus praecox
Cornus mas
Daphne mezereum
Eranthis hyemalis
Erica carnea
Erica x darleyensis
Galanthus
Hamamelis
Helleborus
Iris ungucularis
Jasminum nudiflorum
Lonicera fragrantissima
Lonicera x purpusii
Lonicera standishii
Mahonia
Sarcococca
Viburnum x bodnantense
Viburnum farreri
Viburnum tinus

Autumn color

There are still a large number of plants in flower during autumn, but the real essence of autumn is the changing color of the foliage. In a small garden it is impossible to have a mass of autumnal trees, but there are quite a number of small trees and bushes that give great pleasure at this time of year. Similar color can be provided in the autumn by berries and fruit. These not only provide wonderful color but also food for birds and small mammals throughout the autumn and winter.

Winter-flowering plants

Many gardeners are unaware of the range of flowering plants that are available during the winter months. Many are highly fragrant, as they need to attract the few insects that are around. Most make good cut flowers for the house.

Extending the season

Try to use shrubs and trees that have more than one season. Many will produce a blaze of color from changing leaves in the autumn, and some will also produce a flush of colorful berries (above). At the other end of the year, bulbs, such as these snowdrops and crocuses (left), can be planted in gaps between other plants as they die back below ground soon after flowering.

the edible garden

There is nothing quite like vegetables and fruit fresh from the garden. Most garden vegetables are selected for flavor, while those sold in shops are bred for other qualities, such as their ability to be transported without bruising their good looks, and their ability to mature at the same time for ease of harvest; flavor comes low on the list. However, vegetable growing takes time, and providing all of the family vegetables for a whole year requires a lot of space. That said, a surprising amount can be grown even in a small garden.

What is needed
Most gardens can grow vegetables. Most need sunny conditions and soil that is not sodden but reasonably moisture retentive. The more fertile the soil the better, so add in as much well-rotted organic material (garden compost or farmyard manure) as possible.

Too big
Some vegetables take up too much space and are best grown on a separate plot or in a large garden. Rows of peas and beans take up a lot of space but can be grown up teepees made of canes or strings. Potatoes are space-hungry, but fortunately, they are cheap to buy and so their space is better used for other vegetables. Rhubarb, asparagus, and globe artichokes are all desirable, but they need a lot of space.

Winter supplies
Vegetables often mature at the same time and it is not possible to eat them all. Why not freeze what you cannot eat for use in the winter? Vegetables such as onions, potatoes, carrots, and other root crops can be stored in a garage or shed. The onions should be hung in skeins or nets, while the root crops can be stored in just-moist sand.

Growing bags
Quite a number of vegetables can be grown in growing bags set on a patio against a wall rather than in the ground. These bags contain compost plus specially formulated fertilizer suitable for growing such plants as tomatoes, peppers, eggplant, beans, lettuces, and more. It is essential that they are watered regularly, at least once a day in hot, dry weather.

Herb pots
There is no reason why herbs cannot be grown in the ground. Herbs growing in pots are both well-producing and decorative. But to save space you can grow them in pots instead. Many herbs, such as chives and sage, can be grown in flower beds, as they are ornamental as well as useful.

Fruit
Fruit can take up a lot of space, but if trees and shrubs are grown as cordons, fans, or espaliers up against walls or fences then they are using up unproductive space and are well worth the effort. It is necessary to net the plants as the fruit ripens or the birds will make off with more than their share.

Delicious fruit
There is nothing quite like ripe fruit picked straight from the plant. Among the easiest to grow in a small garden is the strawberry. It can be grown in a small bed or in a container of some sort. Most people grow the lush, large strawberries, but why not grow a few of the small but delicious wild strawberries?

▶ ▶ Also see: The nature garden, pages 42–43

Best value for space

Beets
Carrots
Dwarf beans
Kohlrabi
Leeks
Lettuce
Radishes
Sprouting broccoli
Tomatoes
Zucchini

Herbs worth growing

Basil
Bay
Chives
Marjoram
Mint
Parsley
Rosemary
Sage
Tarragon

Home produce
There is no reason why the small gardener should not grow a few vegetables. Many, such as this cabbage, are decorative as well as edible. Various herbs can also be grown to great advantage in a small garden, either in a bed or in containers. Place containers as close as possible to the kitchen door for convenience.

nature garden

Looking after your own

To be a good gardener you have to learn to work with nature and not against it. Natural areas in the garden give a home to wildflowers, while ponds provide water sources for birds and small mammals, and attract dragonflies and many other insects, as well as frogs and newts. Trees and shrubs also provide essential food, shelter, and nesting sites for birds.

Close to nature

Apart from occasional excursions to the countryside, most people's closest contact with nature is in their garden. Many watch birds and mammals from the window or look at butterflies flitting between flowers in the summer. The gardener is in a unique position. Working with the soil, letting it run through the fingers, constantly looking at plants, in bushes, and under stones, the gardener is much more aware of the life that lives or passes through the garden. Even the weather comes under closer scrutiny than most people give it.

Educational Opportunities

One big advantage of encouraging wildlife in the garden is that children can experience it firsthand and can be encouraged to respect and, indeed, not be frightened of it. The unknown is often the cause of fear, and fluttering birds, flee-ridden hedgehogs, slimy slugs, or hopping frogs can all be terribly frightening if you are not familiar with them. Wild animals are not pets and should not be treated as such, but there is no harm in watching them and very occasionally handling them.

It is extremely important to get to know the world in which we live. Encourage children to read about wildlife and keep records of all the animals and birds that they see. Once discovered, the pleasures of nature will stay with a child for life.

Conservation

In the increasingly concrete world in which we live, any area of greenery is most welcome to wildlife. Within minutes of filling a pond with water, for example, pond-loving insects are likely to appear. Even creating an ordinary garden will attract a large number of insects and birds, but by selecting plants carefully, food and shelter that might otherwise not be available can be supplied for a harsh winter.

Protecting wildlife

Conservation is not all about encouraging wildlife, it is also about protecting it. Life is a very complex business, with various aspects interacting in unforeseeable ways. Kill off one aspect, either deliberately or accidentally, and the effects can snowball so that animals and plants that seem to have no connection to one another suddenly disappear. Whole-scale use of chemicals have caused such reactions, and many gardeners have now turned against using them because they are not certain of the long-term effects. Fortunately, it is perfectly possible to garden without the use of chemicals, or at the least using only those that occur naturally.

Feeding the birds

If you become involved in feeding birds, it's a commitment you need to keep. Birds need to be fed consistently, because they will rely on this food source, so don't put out food for them one day and not the next. Once they begin to rely on your hospitality it is essential that you keep providing it. By all means, keep pets, but do not encourage birds to feed on the lawn and then suddenly introduce a cat! If you do later decide to take in a cat as a pet, the best time to bring it to the house is in late summer when fewer birds will be coming to feeding stations.

Helping hand
Creating a habitat in which nature thrives is not only satisfying but also increasingly important for the survival of both animals and plants. For example, as the number of farm ponds have declined with the demise of the working horse, the garden pond has become one of the main breeding sites for frogs.

encouraging wildlife

Although there are very few places on earth where something living does not occur, some places are more favored than others. These tend to be places where conditions are particularly suitable for life to thrive. If you create suitable conditions where birds and animals will find food, shelter, and nesting sites, then they will adopt your garden. If your garden area has been covered in concrete, they will look elsewhere.

Some berried plants
Berberis
Chaenomeles
Cotoneaster
Crataegus
Daphne
Euonymus europaeus
Hippohae rhamnoides
Ilex
Ligustrum
Malus
Rosa
Sorbus
Symphoricarpos
Viburnum opulus

Some bee and butterfly plants
Aster
Buddleia
Calamintha
Centranthus ruber
Cephalaria
Coreopsis
Cotoneaster
Echinacea
Echinopsis
Erigeron
Eryngium
Escallonia
Hebe
Hedera
Helenium
Hesperis matronalis
Lavandula
Mentha
Nepeta
Salvia
Scabiosa
Sedum
Solidago
Thymus

Wild food
One way of encouraging wildlife to come to the garden as well as helping wildlife to survive is to provide food and shelter. You can offer bags of nuts, but it is better to grow shrubs and other plants that provide a natural source of food. Here, a squirrel eats a nut fallen from a hazel bush, while below, berberis berries await the birds' attention.

Changing style
Adopting a policy of encouraging wildlife is not at odds with wanting a beautiful garden; in fact, the two often go together. Everyone benefits from diversity in the garden.

Food
Food can be provided for wildlife either by putting it out in the garden or by planting plants that will provide food in a more natural way. Bird feeders are a simple way of encouraging birds to the garden. For a more natural source of food, plant bushes that will provide berries for autumnal and winter use. Also leaving the dead stems on herbaceous plants will provide plenty of seeds and shelter for insects that birds will seek out.

▶ ▶ Also see: Ponds and streams, pages 50–51

Flower power

Flowering plants provide food for a number of insects that come to collect pollen and nectar. Bees, butterflies, and many other insects are attracted to the garden by particular plants and are beneficial to the garden. Old-fashioned flowers, rather than modern cultivars (or hybrids) are best for this as hybrids often lack nectar.

Shelter

In addition to food, birds and other animals need shelter and nesting sites. Shrubs and trees provide these, particularly those with dense, tangled stems. In an area with small gardens, persuade a neighbor to plant a few shrubs just over the fence from your own few shrubs. Between the two of you, you will create a much bigger haven. If you have trees that provide no opportunity for birds to build nests, provide nest boxes.

Water

Ponds are a magnet for wildlife of all sorts. They not only provide drink for most types of animals but also a home for a great deal of insect and aquatic life. Colorful dragonflies are always welcome. Fish are a bit more problematic. Unless the pond is a large one, they tend to eat most other aquatic life, usually while it is still at its egg or juvenile stage, negating the purpose of the pond. If you want fish, be sure you do not overstock your pond.

Sweet nectar
One of the greatest joys of the garden is having butterflies adopt it as their home. They will only do this if there is a diversity of plants that produce nectar. Many of the old-fashioned or meadow flowers are best for this.

organic gardening

Nature against nature
As well as making a delightful garden, a wide range of flowering plants also helps to attract ladybugs, hoverflies, and other beneficial insects that prey on greenfly and other pests. In this way the gardener achieves a balance between good and bad insects and never has to spray against infestations of the latter.

Thankfully, the days when gardeners spent most of their time spraying chemicals over everything either to kill it or to make it grow are virtually over. Sprays are still used, but in a more responsible fashion, and they are safer on the whole. Many gardeners now realize that it is unnecessary to spray every time a bug or weed appears in the garden. Many slight problems or infestations can be tolerated as they cause little or no damage. Problems are considerably reduced by using a variety of flowering plants, especially heirlooms, which that encourage hoverflies and ladybugs, both of which prey on aphids.

What's in the soil?

There seems to be almost universal agreement now that well-rotted organic material is the best possible conditioner for soils. It not only provides nutrients but also improves the structure of the soil. While chemical foods provide an instant fix, they do little for the soil.

Composts

Compost all garden waste and any leaves that you can collect, as well as any uncooked vegetable waste from the kitchen. Do not raid your local woods or the woodland habitat will be destroyed, and be careful not to add pernicious weeds to the compost. Either make your own compost bins or buy a ready-made one.

Types of compost

	Advantages	Disadvantages
Farmyard manure	Excellent soil conditioner and nutrient provider	Not always easy to acquire, may contain weed seed
Leaf mold	Excellent soil conditioner and nutrient provider	Usually only available in small quantities
Garden compost	Made at home, so readily available; recycles materials	May contain weed seed if not properly made
Proprietary manures	Excellent soil conditioner and nutrient provider, convenient	Expensive
Seaweed	Excellent soil conditioner and nutrient provider	Only locally available, except in small quantities

Weeds

The real secret is to keep on top of weeds and remove any that appear by hand. It is more difficult when clearing land for the first time. Smothering them with black polyethylene (plastic) is one of the most effective methods if the soil is too heavy to remove the weeds by hand while digging.

Slugs and snails

Not all animals are welcome in the garden. Slugs and snails are probably the least well-liked. In the past, the remedy has been to smother the garden with slug pellets, but these can be injurious to both pets and wildlife. The best way of reducing the problem to manageable proportions is to go out at night with a flashlight and collect them while they are feeding on your plants and move them to another site, preferably a long way from your garden. There are other traditional methods, but this is the most effective.

Waste not
The addition of compost to the soil not only creates a better texture but also adds nutrients, thus reducing or eliminating the need to use chemical fertilizers. Compost bins can easily be constructed and can be used to recycle all organic waste from the garden and any uncooked vegetable waste, such as peelings, from the kitchen.

wild water

Water features

There is nothing quite like having water in the garden; it adds another dimension altogether. Even a small pool, perhaps one contained in a half-barrel, will provide a habitat for a few water plants, as well as creating attractive reflections that always draw the eye. Moving water, either in a stream or from a fountain or spout, adds even more interest. The tinkling or tumbling sound is very restful and helps to create a sense of peace and tranquility in a garden, even if there is the roar of traffic in the background. The movement also creates a restless surface, with reflections being thrown off in all directions.

Good, bad, or indifferent

Of all the features in a garden, those incorporating water are the most likely to be mishandled and to turn out to be an eyesore rather than a stunning attraction. Often, the idea is sound but the execution takes a little extra planning. There is nothing worse than a half-empty pond with a few sad, marooned plants and a heavily creased liner showing above the water line. Think and plan carefully before you start. Take advice and use professional help if need be and the result will certainly be worthwhile.

Style

There is a world of difference between a formal pond and a natural one. When you are designing the garden, decide what you want to achieve, what style of water feature will best suit the overall design of the garden. In a small, paved garden, for example, a formal design will be better than trying to create a miniature natural pond. On the other hand, in a larger garden, where the arrangement of plants is freer flowing, a natural pond may well be better suited. In many cases, a semi-formal pond, one with hard edges that is freely planted, is likely to be the best choice. Unlike borders, ponds and other water features are difficult and expensive to change once they are installed, so plan carefully.

Moving water

It is a lucky gardener who has a natural stream running through the grounds. However, with ingenuity, it is possible to create a stream that looks natural. But again, nothing looks sadder than a badly constructed stream. The best streams are not those that take over the whole garden but those that are part of an overall design. A short stream tumbling down waterfalls in a rock garden to a pool at the base can be very attractive.

Plants

A formal water feature, if of a strong enough design, can stand on its own, but most need to have plants associated with them to look at their best. Even fountains and spouts can benefit from having at least some greenery around them, planted in pots if the surrounding area is paved. If there are fish in ponds or pools it is essential that oxygenating plants be used. It is equally important that there are clear areas with no plants.

Maintenance

Ponds and other water features do need to be maintained. Keep leaves and debris out of the water and every so often either empty the pond and clean it out or carefully dredge the bottom. Great care must be taken if the pond has a liner as they are easy to puncture. Do not allow plants to take over the pond or pool. Regularly remove any excess.

Tranquil water
A pool of water, no matter how small, and its surrounding plants add a touch of tranquility to a garden. A pool also provides drinking water and habitat for many animals. Creating a small pool opens up a whole range of beautiful plants. Any extra work involved in creating and maintaining a pool is far outweighed by the pleasure it gives.

ponds and streams

Informal pools
Ponds that are fully integrated into the design of the garden work best. Above, the water cascades down into a rocky pool that merges into the lawn. Wooden decking (right) allows an intimate view of the water and its contents without looking at all intrusive. Small trees and other plants soften the edges of both pools and helps them blend into the landscape.

Ponds and streams are fun to construct but they must be properly made if they are to be successful. Do not skimp on either time or materials.

Design under water

Just as the overall design of the pond in respect to the garden as a whole must be taken into consideration, the underwater profile of the pond should be considered. Aquatic plants like different depths of water. Therefore, it is a good idea to create a series of ledges or steps around the pond so that planting baskets can be placed at the appropriate depth. A further consideration is to have a gradual slope in some part of the pond so that animals can easily reach the water's edge and birds have shallow water in which to bathe.

Installing flexible liners

Dig a hole for the final shape of the pond and line it with a soft sand. Lay the liner across the pond, held taut around its edges with bricks or stones. With a hose pour water onto the liner. As it fills, the liner will gradually sink into the pond, taking up the excavated shape. Trim off the excess liner and bury the edges beneath the surrounding bank or under edging stones.

Planting ponds

Unless you have a puddled clay pond it is impossible to plant aquatic plants directly into the pond as there is no access to soil. The way to get around this is to use lattice pots that are designed for ponds. Special pond potting compost should be used, as ordinary compost is likely to float away unless held in place by a layer of gravel.

 ▶ ▶ Also see: Encouraging wildlife, pages 44–45

Pond and Stream Liners

	Advantages	Disadvantages
Polyethylene	Cheap	Short life, difficult to install
PVC	Flexible, fits any shape of pool, easy to install	Superseded by LDPE, easily punctured
LDPE	Very flexible, fits any shape of pool, easy to install	Easily punctured
Butyl	Best flexible liner, easy to install, blends in well, relatively long life	Expensive, easily punctured
Rigid	Cheap, preformed	Fixed designs, limited sizes
Sectional	Rigid construction, but sections allow greater range of sizes	Still limitations in design
Concrete	Allows any shape to be made, long life	Can crack if not installed correctly, expensive
Puddled clay	Forms a natural pond, plants can be planted directly into it	Needs source of clay, must not dry out as it will crack

Formal pools

Above: In more formal situations pools with clear-cut lines are preferable. Here, the circular pond works well between the paved area and the cropped lawn. The formality has been toned down by the large amount of diverse foliage floating and growing in the water.

Streams

Streams should look as natural as possible. They can emerge from one pool and descend to another or appear as a spring from under a rock to fall down to a pool. Pumps are available to lift the water to create either a trickle or a torrent. Concrete makes a better liner than a flexible one unless the latter is really well disguised. Concrete soon takes on a natural, rocky appearance, especially if it has stones embedded in it.

Frozen ponds

If you have fish it is not a good idea to let the pond freeze over as gases will build up and oxygen will be depleted. A pond heater will keep a small amount of surface area unfrozen. If you do not have a heater, stand a pan of hot water on the ice to create a hole. Do not break the ice as the shock waves may damage the fish.

Concrete pools can be harmed by the pressure of ice. Rubber balls or lumps of polystyrene placed in the water will help absorb the pressure.

fountains and spouts

Fountains and water spouts are ideal for small gardens, especially if there is no room for a pond or if open water is a potential hazard because of young children. One of the great things about falling water, besides its sparkle and reflections, is the soothing tinkling sound that it makes. Although it may require a bit of time and effort to set up, the results are certainly worth it.

Tiny bubbles
Bubble fountains (above) not only make an interesting use of water, but also are safe for children as there is no pool of water above ground. Traditional fountains (right) create a wonderful focal point in the garden and add the delightful sound of tinkling water and sparkling patterns of reflected light.

Fountains
A large range of different fountains is now available. Fountains can be used as part of a pool or pond, or they can be the sole purpose of the set-up with the pool being part of the fountain. There are a large number of different spray patterns to choose from, some fountains offering several alternatives. It is also possible to get fountains that will automatically change their spray patterns every few seconds.

Not all fountains need pools. The bubble fountain, where water bubbles out of a stone or the ground, is frequently set in a bed of large pebbles with the reservoir and pump hidden below. These are not only very attractive, especially in the small garden, but they are also safe if there are young children around.

Wind
When setting up a fountain, remember to take into account the strength of the wind. In a windy site a tall jet may be constantly blown away from the pool so that the water falls outside. If strong winds are only a periodic nuisance, a tall jet can be switched off for the duration, but if winds are frequent, choose a smaller jet.

 ▶ ▶ Also see: The Nature garden, pages 42–43

Spouts

Spouts are single jets of water emitted from a pipe in a wall or column, falling into a basin, pool, or onto rocks or pebbles. There are many designs of spouts now available, but some of the most popular are no more than a mask, of a lion, for example, that is fixed to a wall in which there is concealed pipework descending to a pump and the pool. They are simple and relatively cheap, but very effective.

Pumps

Pumps are quite inexpensive and available in a wide range. The more powerful the pump the bigger the possible jet. Most pumps are submersible and are kept in the pond immediately below the fountain, but for bigger fountains the pump is kept in pump chambers. Electricity and water is a dangerous mix, so get professional help if you have any doubt whatsoever about the installation of pumps or underwater lights.

Something different

With modern electronics, the old art of trick fountains can be carried further than was ever imaginable. This type of fountain is often made to turn on suddenly, and can be startling. Using what are called "magic eyes" as switches, a row of fountains can be made to turn on and off as a person walks along the path, or a the fountain can spring into action as a visitor approaches it. With more expensive equipment they can even be made to dance to music or make complicated patterns. Lighting a fountain from below can create magical effects.

Spouting spouts
Water spouts have been used to create humorous situations in gardens for centuries. Not all spouts need be as entertaining as the one pictured here, but they can still be relied upon to create interest and to add another dimension to a garden that only water can provide.

exotica

Living on the wild side

One advantage a small garden has over a larger one, especially if enclosed, is that it can easily be transformed into an exotic oasis. This works particularly well on a small scale. The extravagance of exotic plants creates a garden unlike any other type, dripping with foliage and mystery.

What is exotica?

Exotic plants are classed as any plants that are not native. Most plants that are grown in gardens come from other countries. Exotic plants on the whole tend to be big, flamboyant ones that often have their origins in the tropics, or at least have the appearance of such. Large specimens of many of the plants may be quite expensive, but many types can be very easily be grown from seed as annuals. Others are simply nothing more than basic houseplants, available from any good florist or garden center.

Exotic gardens

The overall effect of an exotic garden is almost that of a jungle, with masses of foliage, much of it large leaved, with occasional splashes of vivid colors. Lit from below at night the garden has an eerie richness. It does not have the tranquillity of a romantic garden, but its grandeur is such that it transports one away from the everyday world. Many of the plants that can be used for this type of garden are tender and will not withstand the winter's extreme frosts. However, they are perfectly happy outside during the summer and can either be grown as annuals or grown in containers and moved inside during the colder months.

Indoors or out

This kind of garden can be created either indoors or out. One of the best ideas is to link the house and the garden. A hot, steamy conservatory can house exotic plants throughout the year, with no change in the seasons, just as in the tropics. The conservatory, or glass house, is used during the winter months and then the doors are thrown open and the inside merges with the outside as the exuberant growth continues into the garden. This is by far one of the best types of design for fully integrating the house and the garden.

Winter days

With the use of conservatories or garden rooms, the illusion of eating and relaxing outside can be carried out throughout the year. Cane or cast iron furniture, frequently painted white, is the traditional furnishing against the backdrop of the rich foliage. It is also a good idea to consider including water elements such as pools and fountains to add to the ambience.

Can exotic gardens grow anywhere?

Outdoor exotic gardens are best where temperatures are at least relatively mild and there is reasonable rainfall. In cold areas they are really only going to be a summer garden, but then it is unlikely that much time would be spent outside anyway during harsh winters. There is no reason why an exotic garden cannot be kept anywhere under glass as long as it is possible to heat it.

Grass roots
Exotica exists in many forms. It can be brash and colorful or it can simply be different and unusual. Grasses are common enough, but used in this way against a background of bamboo they create a wild, lush image that is very exotic in its appeal.

under glass

Many gardeners see the greenhouse as a means to an end, a place to propagate plants for the garden or to raise tomatoes and cucumbers. Others see them in a completely different light. For them greenhouses are places to keep exotic plants or to grow various plants and vegetables and keep them on shelves. Some people use a greenhouse to create more of an indoor garden. With a conservatory, a greenhouse attached to the house, you can create a stunning indoor garden to enjoy throughout the year.

Temperatures

It is important to decide whether the conservatory is simply for plants or also for living in, and what types of plants will be grown, as much will depend on this. For living and entertaining, the temperature should not be too high and the humidity should be low. Tropical plants, on the other hand, need higher temperatures and high humidity to do well. Plenty of plants do not have these requirements and an effective garden room can still be created. If your heart is set on growing tropical plants it may be possible to divide the conservatory in two, keeping one part hotter than the other. Alternatively, it is always possible to install a greenhouse within the conservatory!

Heating

If the exotic garden is created within a conservatory then it may be possible to extend the house's central heating into it; if not, independent heaters will be required. These can be simple electric heaters, or a hot water or air system can be run from a small boiler. The air may be too dry for many plants and it may be necessary to include a humidifier in the system. Alternatively, pools with waterfalls or fountains can be used to help to keep the air moist.

Greenhouses

There is nothing wrong with using a greenhouse in a more conventional manner, for growing potted plants to take into the house when they are in flower, for propagating plants, and for growing crops such as tomatoes or grapes.

It is easier to grow exotic plants in a greenhouse as it does not usually serve the dual function of housing people as well as plants. Temperature and humidity can therefore be maintained to serve the plants rather than people. There is also no need to create an aesthetic garden, as such; plants can be arranged more for convenience than for show. However, it is just as easy to turn a greenhouse into a garden feature. Once climbers begin to hang from the roof it quickly becomes an interesting place.

Maintenance

Watering and feeding are the keys to success. Under heated glass, the compost in which the plants are growing can dry out very quickly. Using automatic watering systems, including standing plants on capillary matting, will make life considerably easier. Because of the amount of watering required, nutrients are leached from the compost very quickly and the plants

will need feeding at least once a week during the growing period.

Shade is something else to take seriously. Most tropical plants are shielded from the sun by the tall forest above them. Blinds are needed in both greenhouses and conservatories to shelter the plants from the steady heat of the sun.

The third requirement is ventilation. Even though the houses must be kept warm, it is also important that the plants receive adequate ventilation; stagnant air promotes disease. The warm, moist conditions are ideal for both disease and pests. One way to avoid both is by having scrupulous hygiene. Remove any rotting vegetation or dead leaves as soon as you see them. Tackle any outbreaks of pests or diseases as soon as you notice them, before they take hold.

Controlled exotica

For a more controlled exotic interior, plants are grouped in containers, creating islands of greenery. The overall effect is of lush, cool foliage, although the temperature can become quite high.

exotic plants

Exotic plants should remind one of tropical gardens, but most exotics are plants that happily grow in far more temperate climates. Bamboos, for example, have a certain exotic appeal, but many are perfectly hardy, as are ferns. While it is possible to use tropical climbers inside, it is often difficult to use them in the open garden.

Orchids rule
Orchids are among the most popular flowers of all time. Although there are many hardy species, it is the more tropical varieties, such as this Phalaeapsis hybrid, that most people like to grow in their conservatory or greenhouse.

Key points

Watering
Feeding
Heating
Shading
Ventilation
Hygiene

Orchids
The one plant that nearly everybody likes to grow is the orchid. While there are a few that can be grown outside, these are not particularly exotic. It is the tropical orchids that capture people's imagination, and these must be grown indoors. Growing orchids can become obsessive and rather expensive, so think carefully before letting them take over your lives. On the other hand, you could end up with a hobby for life.

Houseplants
Many houseplants make perfect specimens for use in an exotic garden, both inside and out. During summer, move some of the houseplants outside; they will not only enjoy the conditions, but it will also provide an exotic touch to the patio. Aspidistras, coleus, spider plants, and many others can all be moved outside as long as the nighttime temperature does not fall too low, say not below about 60 degrees.

Climbers and trailers
Plants that climb and trail are important to the overall effect in an exotic garden. Hothouse plants such as glory lily (Gloriosa) and Split-leaf philodendron (Monstera deliciosa), can be used in heated conservatories, but outside, substitutes must be used. Simple ivy (Hedera) is extremely effective and is also tough enough to withstand battering winds. Passion flowers (Passiflora) have very exotic flowers and fruit and are hardy, particularly if grown against a wall. For real color in the conservatory, try bougainvillea.

Foliage
Ferns, hostas, bamboos, and phormiums are all hardy plants that can be used, although there are tender examples of them that can be grown inside. Fatsia japonica, various rubber plants (Ficus), and bananas (Musa) are shrubby examples. Many flowering plants, camellias and cannas for example, have excellent foliage. Some can be grown regularly from seed. The castor bean plant, Ricinus communis, is a good example of one with excellent foliage.

 ▶ ▶ Also see: Romantic planting, pages 26–27

Flower power

Orchids, as has been mentioned, are fabulous additions to an exotic garden. Others include Datura or brugmansia, magnificent plants with a heady scent. Strelitzia has a very exotic look, but so then do lots of relatively common plants, like busy lizzies and impatiens.

Desert days

Above: Desert plants of various types add a different exotic dimension to many gardens and conservatories. They have the advantage of not needing much attention, and needing far less watering and feeding than the more lush, tropical exotica.

Hardy and tender

Left: An exotic garden is created from a mixture of hardy and tender plants. The bright, brash colors are set off well against the luxuriant foliage, giving a tropical feeling to the scene. Foliage plays a very important part in exotic gardens, and attention should be given to choosing plants with interesting shapes, color, and texture.

Bigger is better

Few gardeners are content with the size of their garden. Most feel they want something larger. However, with a bit of design trickery it is possible to make the garden look much bigger than it really is. Even a small basement garden can appear to be doubled in size with a little bit of effort.

There are other tricks that help to draw the eye where the gardener wants it to go, be it toward something attractive or away from something unsightly. It is also possible to help make an immature garden appear as if it has been there for some time.

Instant gardens

When moving into a new house, many people want their gardens to look good as quickly as possible; they want an instant garden. It takes a while to establish a garden, but if you are prepared to go out and buy mature plants, it is possible to fill up a garden very quickly. It is often a good idea to live with a garden for a while before deciding what you want to do with it. In the meantime, why not use plants in pots? A magnificent display can be created using containers as temporary plantings. The plants can be bright annuals, perennials, or shrubs. Both the perennials and shrubs can be used in the ground when the garden has been established.

Annuals

For a splash of color, fill any existing borders with annuals, either using established plants or by just scattering packets of seed, a less expensive method. If there are no borders, dig some temporary ones.

Instant pathways

Laying paving and other solid surfaces takes time and can be quite expensive. There are ways, however, to lay surfaces either for paths or a terrace in a comparatively short time. Gravel, available in bags, is a magnificent boon to the instant garden. First, prepare the surface, tamp it down, and then pour the gravel over it. This very attractive surface can be used as soon as it is laid. The gravel will get pushed down into the soil and some areas will eventually wear thin, but a new bag of gravel tipped over it will refresh it in a matter of seconds. Another option for quick surfaces is to create a softer surface with tanbark.

Instant lawns

Sown lawns take a while to become mature enough for any activity to take place on them. Sod lawns come into use much more quickly. However, if you use sod, don't be tempted to skimp on the preparation; it is important to make certain that the site is level and that all perennial weeds have been removed or they will only regrow and become hopelessly mixed into the lawn.

In the meantime

Once you start to establish a garden using a finished design, it will take a some time to mature and grow to fill the space. It is a good idea to fill in the gaps with annuals or temporary plantings so that the immature shrubs and perennials do not look lost in a sea of soil. As well as creating a visual effect, the annuals will also act as a ground cover and help keep the growth of weeds to a minimum.

Seeing is believing
A small garden can be extended way beyond its boundaries with the aid of the paintbrush. This town garden looks out onto a mythical countryside that only exists in the eye of the beholder. The use of trompe-l'oeil is a skilled art but one that can really enhance a garden.

creating focal points

Focal points are essential components of garden design. Consider positioning a particular plant or garden object in a way that catches the eye.

Drawing the eye

There are several reasons for using focal points in a garden. One is simply to draw attention to a particularly attractive feature. A focal point in a border tends to break the monotony and add interest. One very useful application of a focal point is to draw the eye away from something else. A container of bright flowers will make the viewer ignore an adjacent border that has finished flowering; a fountain will keep the eye from wandering off to a neighbor's unsightly garage that shows above the hedge. If the focal point is at the end of a path or lawn, it helps give the impression that the garden is bigger than it is, as it draws the eye past everything else.

Structures

Summer houses and gazebos make good focal points. People are always attracted to them even if they do not linger there for long. The higher quality the design the better, as they are a prominent feature if they are used as a focal point. Place structures at the end of a broad path or on an edge of the lawn. Hidden in the trees or shrubs they make quite a different point and a less expensive type can be used.

Furniture

Furniture such as a humble bench can be a draw in a garden. A white wooden or iron seat at the end of a curve in a path will attract the eye. Once a person is seated, the eye passes back along the vista. This can make a very restful place to sit.

Sculpture

Reproduction sculpture is widely available and relatively cheap. Original sculpture is far more expensive but usually much more interesting and satisfying. Again, good positions are generally at the end of paths or lawns, but they also work very well partly submerged in foliage, particularly amongst shrubs.

Containers

Large containers such as urns can be used instead of sculpture, especially if they are stood on plinths. They are very effective at drawing the eye, particularly at the end of or at a bend in a path. Smaller containers of plants can be placed in borders where flowers are beginning to fade to perk them up and create something of interest for the eye.

Using plants

The cheapest method of creating a focal point is with a plant. If it is part of a planted area it has to be a plant that is decidedly different from its neighbors or it will disappear into the background. A bright yellow lily growing amongst the green foliage of a shrubbery or a blue delphinium amongst a border of yellow flowers will always stand out. Specimen plants standing by themselves will also draw the eye. Pampas grass at the ends of the lawn, perhaps where it catches the evening sun, can be very effective, as can a solitary columnar conifer.

Simple effects
This small garden is made to look much larger by the constriction of the bordered pathway, taking the eye down to a lawn that expands to an unseen size way beyond sight. The small size is further disguised by the eye being drawn into the apparent distance to the focal point of the glistening fountain. This is a good example of simple visual effects increasing the size of the garden.

▶ ▶ Also see: Container planting, pages 12–13; Year-round interest, pages 36–37

Full stops
Remove the urn at the end of this pergola and the result would be a dead-end of no particular significance. Leave the urn where it is and the eye immediately travels toward it, creating a full stop and at the same time enhancing the visual quality of the elegant walkway, although it is in no way physically connected to it.

garden deceits

What the eye does not see

Humans are curious creatures by nature. Curve a pathway out of sight and someone will want to know what lies around the corner. Our minds always seem to imagine that there is something more interesting just out of sight. This is a useful device for increasing the apparent size of a garden. A pathway that disappears around a corner must lead to another part of the garden, even if in reality it leads to a blank wall.

There are various tricks that can be used in gardens to make them appear to be something they are not. Size is usually the main area of deceit, with gardeners wanting to make their gardens appear bigger. Location or setting is another. Once you begin to think creatively, the possibilities are endless.

Mirage

In very small gardens, such as those the size of small basement areas, the size can appear to be doubled by the careful use of one or more mirrors. Unless studying it carefully (or trying to walk through it), anyone looking at the mirror will think they see more garden beyond a doorway or window, when it is in fact the reflection of the garden they are in.

Trompe l'oeil

Another trick is to create a trompe-l'oeil, a French term that means "trick of the eye." In its simplest form, this is just a painting on a wall or fence that is

so lifelike that it looks real. A painting of a doorway with more garden beyond deceives the eye into thinking the garden is much bigger than it really is. A painting with countryside and animals, cows or sheep perhaps, transforms a town garden to a rural one. Sometimes the trompe-l'oeil can be three-dimensional. A popular trick is to fix the trellis to a wall that has a distorted perspective and appears to recede into the distance. Inside the trellis arch there may be a painting to depict what lies through the gap, or even a mirror to offer a view into a neighbor's garden (which is not trickery, but cheating!).

 ▶ ▶ Also see: Disguising essentials, pages 122–123

Creating a bigger lawn

Mowing the lawn in stripes that go away from the viewer will make the lawn look much longer. With the lines going across the grass, the lawn will seem shorter.

Longer paths

A similar effect can be obtained with brick paths by laying the bricks length-ways along the path; this draws the eye ever onwards, giving the impression that the path is much longer than it is. Place the bricks horizontally across the path and the eye is stopped as if by a barrier and the path seems shorter.

Using color

The use of pale colors, especially misty blues at the end of a border, will make the border look farther away than it is (in the same way that hills look farther away on a misty day than on a bright one). Conversely, bright reds will seem to be closer than their true position.

Disappearing into the unknown

Another trick to consider when laying out the garden is to ensure that it is not possible to see the everything in one glance. Design the garden in such a way that paths curve away behind shrubs or trellises to create the impression that the garden goes on and on, out of sight. Skillfully handled, it should be possible to have somebody walk in a circle, around the whole garden, thinking that they still have not gotten to the end of it yet.

A shining example
Mirrors are excellent devices for increasing the size of a garden; they are unexpected and easily fool people into misinterpreting what they see. This one, placed at the end of a small pool, reflects the garden in such a way that it seems to carry on beyond the boundary. Softening the edges of the mirror with trellising and climbers helps disguise it.

arches and trellises

A flat, two-dimensional garden is generally rather uninteresting. Once it is lifted into the third dimension with shrubs and small trees it starts to become far more interesting. However, trees and shrubs take time to grow and mature. An immediate way to gain height is to erect trellising. Trellising serves several important functions. First, it is a support for climbers, a very important group of plants. These not only increase the height of the garden by taking the plants upwards, but also act as screens. Second, arches provide the means for moving from one area to the next. And last, they provide screens, a very important part of any garden.

Framing
As well as physically supporting gates, arches have a very important visual role. They frame a section of what lies beyond and thus entice the viewer to enter. The framing can be a simple arch such as brick or hedging, but the structure becomes very attractive if used to support climbing plants, such as the roses seen here.

Internal screens
Plant screens are useful for preventing the eye from seeing all of the garden at once, but at the same time, they provide tantalizing glimpses of what lies beyond. Breaking a garden, even a small one, into several compartments or individual gardens with the use of screens makes a garden far more interesting and also makes it seem larger.

Internal screens have another benefit: they not only deflect the eye, but they also deflect the wind. In breezy areas, the more hedges and trellises there are, the less damage the wind will cause.

Boundary screens
Boundary screens also help greatly with the problem of reducing wind damage. In addition, they give privacy from prying eyes and they can help block out noise. It is quicker to grow plants over trellising than it is to grow a hedge, and it is also more colorful.

Arches
Arches are wonderful in the garden. They are the means by which one moves from one area to another. One can glimpse the next area of the garden as one walks through the garden, but not all is revealed until one passes through the arch. Arches also act as supports for climbing plants, so that the passage from one area to the next is a pleasant one, especially if the flowers are fragrant. Arches are available in many different designs, from formal to rustic, and they can be purchased readymade or homemade.

Plants for arches and trellises
Clematis
Cobaea scandens
Humulus
Ipomoea
Lathyrus odoratus
Lonicera
Rosa
Solanum crispum
Solanum jasminoides
Thunbergia alata
Vitis

► ► Also see: Entrances and exits, pages 88–89; Inner boundaries, pages 120–121

Materials and design

Trellises can be made of plastic or wood. Plastic is really only suitable for very small areas and is preferably attached to walls or solid fences. Wood is far more sympathetic to the garden and is much stronger. There is a very wide range of designs, both in the way the wood overlaps but also in the overall shape of the trellis. The supporting posts usually benefit by some form of finial on their tops.

Arches can be made from wood, but proprietary ones are also made from metal or plastic. Plastic arches may not last for very long. Arches can also be made by extending an adjacent hedge. A more formal arch can be constructed from bricks.

Cool walkways
Pergolas are a series of connected arches, usually covered with climbers and placed along a path or walkway. As well as creating an enticing tunnel of often fragrant flowers, they make a beautiful shaded walkway or even sitting area. Roses, clematis, or plants with large tassels of flowers such as laburnum or wisteria, seen here, are all good candidates for clothing the structure.

Pergolas and walkways

A pergola is a series of arches connected together to form a walkway. It can be kept as a plain structure, but it looks much better if it is covered with climbers. A path disappearing through a pergola tends to make the garden look much bigger and can be a very pleasant way of joining one area to another. Fragrant climbers, such as wisteria, honeysuckle, or roses, are especially good. However, if the pergola is relatively narrow, avoid using prickly roses.

flower power

Flower people

For many people, the purpose of a garden is to have flowering plants. Not everyone would agree, as they do take up a bit more time than, say, just growing shrubs. However, the extra time is well worth it, and it need not be excessive. Annuals and bedding plants, for example, once planted require little time and yet go on cheerfully flowering well into autumn. Perennials tend to have a more restricted flowering period, but this provides the opportunity to have a border or garden that constantly changes in appearance as some plants fade and others come into flower.

Flowers in the garden

How does one fit flowers into the design of a garden? The conventional way is to create a series of borders around a central lawn. This can be attractive, although many people may find it uninteresting. A good alternative is a sinuous path meandering between two borders filled with flowering plants, creating a very pleasant place to wander; one feels more in contact with the flowers than if viewing them from the middle of a lawn. If the garden is very small, flowering plants can be displayed in containers arranged on a patio or used in a more three-dimensional display on the side of steps, or by using hanging baskets or window boxes.

Flowers for color

Choose the combination of flower colors as carefully as you would clothing or room furnishings. The colors should blend together harmoniously, perhaps with the odd bit of discord to enliven things. Softer colors are more restful and easier to combine. Strong colors add a touch of excitement to a garden, especially hot reds and oranges, but keep in mind that too much of a good thing and will soon become boring. Try to blend colors, moving gently from one to another. Avoid dotting different colors all over the place so that the result is spotty; the eye finds it difficult to rest somewhere in a spotty border. Merging patches of color are more harmonious and pleasant to the eye.

Flowers for fragrance

There is a tendency to think of flowers only in terms of color but there is often much more to them. Fragrance is also a quality that endears many kinds of flowers to gardeners. In a small garden every flower should be made to pay its way, and if there is a choice between a flower of a certain color and another flower of the same color but with a perfume, go for the perfumed one every time. There are so many flowers to choose from that the small gardener should usually be able to choose a fragrant one.

Flowers for cutting

One of the nicest things about growing flowers in the garden is that there is always something that can be cut and taken indoors. If possible, devote a small corner for growing flowers just for cutting. The cutting garden can be part of the vegetable garden or can even be in the greenhouse. Many plants can be included in a border. Chrysanthemums and dahlias, for example, are excellent cut flowers and can either be grown in a special area or as part of the colorful scene in a border.

Dried flowers

Some flowers dry better than others, and if a winter arrangement is desired it is worth growing a few plants with this in mind. Potpourri is a wonderful reminder of summers past, and flowers suitable for inclusion in potpourri may also be considered.

Painting with flowers
While foliage gives a garden structure and permanence, flowers add glitter and provide an ever-changing scene. No two days are alike: as more flowers come into bloom, others fade away. As the different varieties come into flower, so the colors change along with shapes and textures. The combinations are infinite and since they are not permanent, the gardener is free to experiment.

bedding plants

For an instant colorful garden, there is nothing quite like annuals and bedding plants. They are cheap, cheerful, and readily available. They can be used in borders, in pots, in hanging baskets, or window boxes, and they last throughout the summer into autumn.

Annuals and bedding plants

Annuals, which also include a number of tender perennials such as pelargoniums, are extremely useful plants in the garden. They come rapidly into flower and last for a very long time, making these ideal for the busy gardener who wants instant results. On the whole they are bright colors and are therefore more suited to a lively color scheme, but they are always guaranteed to brighten up the scene.

Growing from seed

The cheapest way of buying annuals is to buy the seed and grow them yourself. Most packets contain plenty of seed and quite a number of plants can be grown for a small outlay of money. Most annuals prefer to be germinated in a warm environment, which means using a propagator, but in small quantities they can be grown indoors in indirect light and in a warm spot. Some annuals are hardy and can be sown where they are to grow either in the previous autumn or in spring. Tender annuals should only be sown outside once the threat of frost is past.

Buying plants

To save the trouble of growing annuals from seed, purchase them as seedlings or small plants from a nursery or garden center. There is not as wide a selection available as there is of seed, but there is still a fair range to chose from. Be careful not to plant out tender annuals before all frosts have gone or you are likely to have to start again.

Containers

Annuals make superb container plants. There is an ever-increasing range of trailing plants that are suitable for hanging baskets and window boxes, as well as sturdier ones for larger containers that can be put on the patio and elsewhere. Their one drawback is that they need constant watering, usually once a day, and even more frequently in hot, dry weather.

▶ ▶ Also see: Fascinating foliage, page 77; Romantic planting, page 26

Colorful annuals

Ageratum houstonianum
Alonsoa
Antirrhinum majus
Argyranthemum
Bidens ferulifolia
Brachycome iberidifolia
Borago officinalis
Centaurea cyanus
Clarkia
Collinsia bicolor
Cynoglossum
Echium
Helichrysum
Iberis
Impatiens
Lobelia erinus
Lobularia maritima
Nigella damascena
Osteospermum
Pelargonium
Petunia
Phacelia
Rudbeckia
Salvia viridus
Scabiosa
Semperflorens begonia
Senecio cineraria
Tropaeolum
Verbena x hybrida
Viola x wittrockiana

Versatility

A handful of different plants can provide a multitude of colors and can be used in all kinds of different situations. Frequent watering and deadheading is all that is required to keep them fresh for a long period. Seen here are *Petunia* 'Million Bells Blue' (left), *Begonia* 'Love Me' (above top), and impatiens (above) in a container.

Bedding

Bedding schemes have gone a little out of fashion in recent times, but they still have a lot going for them if you like brash colors and a fairly instant garden. One big advantage is that you can have a completely different garden each year simply by changing the colors and the planting plan. Different colors are better planted in blocks rather than planted randomly.

Mixed borders

There is a lot to be said for mixing different types of plants so that you get the best of all worlds. Create a herbaceous and shrub border that provides form and structure. Fill the gaps with annuals for bright and continuous color.

herbaceous plants

Herbaceous plants are perennials. They usually take a year or so to reach their final size, so a border containing them is not as instant as one containing solely annuals. Although there are many brightly colored perennials, on the whole their colors are more subtle than annuals and allow for more variety when designing a border. Generally, perennials are bulkier, more substantial plants and give the border a more solid, three-dimensional appearance. Most do not flower for as a long a period as annuals, but this can be an advantage as it means that the border can be a changing scene. It is possible to get a bit bored with the same annuals all summer and autumn.

Borders

It is in borders that perennials excel. Few small gardeners can hope to have enormous herbaceous borders disappearing into the distance. In a small garden, a surprisingly large number of interesting plants can be packed into a small area or a nice display can be had by using relatively few plants. Most herbaceous perennials are easy to propagate, especially by division. Large stocks can be built up very cheaply to allow them to be planted in quantity for drifts of color.

Colors and shapes
One of the important things about herbaceous perennials is their sheer variety. They come in an infinite range of colors, sizes, shapes, and textures. There are plants for all soils and positions. It is very difficult to imagine gardening without them. Here, herbaceous perennials are planted as solid blocks of color, but there are furry plumes and airy clouds, accented with bright spots of color.

Individual specimen plants

Herbaceous plants are generally thought of as being primarily plants for the border, but they have many other uses. Many make excellent specimen plants either to be used in isolation or to stand out in a border as a focal point. Pampas grass, for example, makes an excellent plant for a central feature on a lawn. Others do well filling an odd corner by themselves in an eye-catching way. *Euphorbia characias wulfenii*, for example, makes a superb green mound with its yellow, flowerlike bracts drawing attention to it for a large part of the year.

Mixed plantings

Perennials mix very well with shrubs and trees. For the modern small garden, this is probably the best combination. The trees and shrubs provide structure and a green environment, while the herbaceous plants produce the color mixed into it. The shrubs ensure that there is something of interest all year.

Containers

Although annuals and tender perennials dominate the container scene, perennials are also often well-suited to containers. Perennials look particularly good when used on their own. For example, a large container of acanthus mollis, a perennial, can look as astounding as can one containing a collection of blue or white agapanthus, an annual.

Easy perennials for cutting

Achillea	Gypsophila
Alstroemeria	Heliopsis
Aster	Liatris
Chrysanthemum	Physalis
Convallaria majalis	Rudbeckia
Dianthus	Solidago
Eryngium	

 ▶ ▶ Also see: Perennials for foliage, pages 78–79; Seasonal plants and shrubs, pages 38–39

Growing perennials

Perennials are not difficult plants to grow as long as the ground is well prepared before they are planted. Some may need staking to prevent them from flopping over in wind or rain, but others require only minimal care—cutting them down in the autumn is the main activity. Some plants are thirstier than others, but it is possible to choose plants that will tolerate a certain amount of drought, minimizing the need to water. If plenty of organic material has been added to the soil before planting and the border is mulched, there should be no need to water at all.

Most perennials benefit from being dug up and divided every four years. Throw away the woody center part of the plants and replant the outer young sections.

Dreamy drifts
One of the best ways of using herbaceous materials is to plant them in blocks, or groups, so that they form drifts of color, that merge into one another.

alpine and rock plants

With the possible exception of roses, there are more gardeners specializing in alpines than any other regional type. Serious alpine gardeners grow a wide range of plants, many of which are ungrowable by those who do not have the required skills. These gardeners grow plants from the high mountain ranges which need very special conditions. At the other extreme, there are gardeners who simply like the effect a rock garden gives to a garden and are content to grow easy but attractive plants in it, such as *Aubrieta deltoidea*. For gardeners who find themselves somewhere in the middle, there are numerous plants that are little known to general gardeners but are attractive and not too difficult to grow.

Common or garden
Rock gardens and other rocky structures need not be devoted to high alpine plants that are difficult to grow. There are plenty of quite common plants, such as this aubrieta deltoidea, that are easy to grow and put on a delightful, colorful display.

Rock gardens
Rock gardens are the primary place for growing alpines. A rock garden is not simply a heap of earth with a few stones dotted on it; it should be properly constructed with a free-draining mixture of loam, grit, and rocks, laid to represent the strata of a rocky outcrop. At least a third of the rock should be buried beneath the soil to provide stability and keep the roots of plants cool. The ledges and vertical crevices between the rocks are planted. Any bare soil mixture is usually covered with a top dressing of gravel or small stones.

Raised beds
Many alpine gardeners are not as interested in the overall effect of their plants as they are concerned with creating the right conditions for each plant to grow. While rock gardens may look pretty, the same conditions can be created by a raised bed with a brick or cement block border filled with the same free-draining mixture. It is easier to tend and, if designed well, can look very attractive.

Troughs
On a smaller scale, many plants are popularly grown in square containers, old animal feeding and drinking troughs made from stone. Old sinks or homemade replicas are also used. These containers are suitable for growing very small alpine plants and for creating miniature landscapes using small pieces of stone for rocks. Again, a very free-draining mixture of good loam and grit is required along with some leaf mold to hold sufficient moisture for the plants.

Easy rock garden plants

Aethionema	Globularia
Anthirrhinum	Leontopodium alpinum
Aquilegia	Linaria alpina
Armeria	Lewisia
Aubrieta deltoidea	Origanum
Aurinia saxatilis	Oxalis
Campanula	Papaver
Daphne	Phlox subulata
Dianthus	Primula
Draba	Saxifraga
Dryas octopetala	Sedum
Erinus alpinus	Sempervivum
Erodium	Silene acaulis
Gentiana	Thymus

▶ ▶ Also see: Fountains and spouts, pages 52–53

Alpine houses

Most alpines are thoroughly hardy, but many are susceptible to damp, mild winters and therefore need some protection, as much from the rain as from the cold. Alpine houses are basically the same as greenhouses except that they have much more ventilation. Even in winter the windows are left open for air to circulate, except when rain or snow is likely to blow in. The staging is usually very strongly constructed as each contains a deep layer of sand into which the pots are sunk. This helps keep the roots warm in winter and cool in summer, and keeps the compost just damp, with moisture creeping in from the sand through the holes in the base of the pot or through the sides of terra cotta pots. Here, some of the most difficult and precious plants are grown.

Alpine glories

The piercing blue of *Gentiana verna* (above) and the delicate poppies *Papaver alpinum* (left) are two of the many rewards of rock gardening. It can be difficult to grow specialist plants, but it can become addictive. It is an ideal form of gardening for the gardener who is short of space but prepared to spend time tending plants.

fascinating foliage

Why focus on foliage?
Many gardens are designed entirely for continuous flowering, but this can become rather overpowering. A well-balanced garden also depends on foliage for its appearance. Foliage not only acts as a foil or a background for flowering plants but is also attractive in its own right.

Shades of green
Although most plants have green leaves, the number of different shades of green seem to be infinite. Many gardeners receive pleasure from this alone. However, there is a very wide range of colors in foliage, from almost white through cream and yellow to gold, and from blue to dusky purple.

Mixed colors
Some of the more interesting leaves are a mixture of two or more colors. Most frequently, mixed-color leaves are green and yellow or cream, but there are also many subtle variations. Variegated foliage is fascinating, but it should be used with care; too much in one place becomes rather messy and unpleasant to look at. It is much better to have one or two well-chosen plants mixed in with normal green foliage. In this way the variegated foliage creates a bigger impact and is better appreciated than if there is a whole patch of it.

Added texture
The texture of leaves is important. Some plants, such as camellias, have shiny leaves which glint in the sunlight and are useful for placing in a dark spot or between dull-leaved shrubs. Other leaves are covered with tiny hairs, giving a velvety look. Lamb's ears (*Stachys byzantina*) are very furry, as their name suggests, giving the plant a rich silver texture.

Interesting shapes
Individual leaves present a great range of shapes and sizes. Gunnera leaves, for example, are similar to the giant rhubarb leaves and have a very dramatic impact, especially in a small garden. Irises and other bulbs produce spiky leaves which make an interesting contrast to, say, the lacy filigree of ferns, or to the more solid foliage of hostas.

Advantageous prickles
The shape of some leaves are enhanced by sharp prickles. Holly, for example, has very interestingly shaped leaves with the margins rising up into sharp needles. The prickles have been developed by the plant to prevent browsing by animals and can still be put to good effect. Holly makes an impenetrable hedge or a wonderful deterrent when grown along a wall.

Foliage gardens
It is possible to have a garden that consists of entirely foliage. With skill, utilizing different colors, shapes, and textures, this could be a very interesting garden, and one that would take little looking after. The most extreme example of this is a garden covered entirely in ivy, which is allowed to creep over everything, including mounds of earth and objects such as tree stumps, giving a three-dimensional effect.

Foliage for cuttings
Foliage is also an important element in flower arranging, especially during winter, when there are few flowers around. When considering which foliage plants to grow this is always worth bearing in mind.

Beautiful foliage
Foliage is often overlooked in a garden where colorful flowers dominate. However, it is worth considering as it can introduce a lot of interest to a garden. Foliage, such as this canna, is often fascinating in its own right, as well as providing a background against which the flowers stand out. Foliage has the advantage that it often lasts longer than flowers and therefore adds a sense of continuity to ever-changing borders.

perennials for foliage

Green filigree
It would be difficult to imagine a garden without ferns. They are among the most handsome of foliage plants and many have the advantage of being able to grow in shady conditions. Many have divided foliage, one of the most delicate being this *Adiantum venustum*. Those with shiny leaves are excellent for brightening up dull spots.

Although mainly thought of as flowering plants, perennials make excellent foliage plants. Many are grown simply for their foliage. Hostas, for example, are grown mainly for the decorative effect of their leaves, although, of course, they also produce flowers.

While some plants are specifically grown for their foliage, many others have a dual purpose. Montbretia (*Crocosmia crocosmiiflora*), which is mainly grown for its orange or yellow flowers, also has very elegant straplike leaves which give interest to borders before and after the flowers bloom. The range of colors, shapes, and textures available in Montbretia is greater than any other group of plants.

Good foliage plants

Acanthus	Foeniculum vulgare
Ajuga	Geranium
Alchmilla	Grasses
Bergenia	Gunnera
Canna	Heuchera
Crocosmia	Hosta
Dicentra	Phormium
Epimedium	Rodgersia
Eryngium	Verbascum
Ferns	Zantedeschia

After flowering

After flowering, many perennials (hardy geraniums, for example), can be cut to the ground. Fresh leaves will appear, allowing them to remain as foliage plants for the rest of the season. Pulmonarias should be pruned as soon as they have finished flowering; they will produce beautiful silver-splashed leaves. If left alone, the foliage of the Pulmonaria will look old and limp and will be an eyesore rather than an attraction.

▶▶ Also see: Herbaceous plants, pages 72–73, Seasonal plants & shrubs, pages 38–39

Color

As with shrubs, perennial plants have a great variety of leaf colors, some variegated, others with simple single colors. The colors should not be used at random but should be seen as part of the overall color scheme of the border, involving the flowers as well. Apart from green, there are very few colors that work as a solid block.

Care should be taken when using several types of variegated plants, with the exception of silver. Silver foliage blends well with a variety of flower colors, and the different textures and leaf shapes allows them to combine together to great effect. Soft pink flowers go especially well with silver, but the combination of silver and bright yellow, although less frequently seen, is also very effective.

Silver foliage

Anaphalis
Artemisia
Celmisia
Centaurea 'Pulchra Major'
Cerastium tomentosum
Cynara cardunculus
Eryngium giganteum
Geranium renardii
Lychnis coronaria
Macleaya
Melianthus major
Onopordum
Romneya coulteri
Santolina
Stachys byzantina
Tanacetum haradjanii

Silver foliage

Above: To many gardeners, the most interesting foliage plants are those with silver leaves. Although they are attractive in their own right, they also work well with a wide range of flower colors, both soft and brash. They are valuable as "linking" plants used to link colors that do not necessarily go well together. Silver plants nearly always like an open, sunny position. They will languish and may eventually die in shade.

Fine foliage

Left: Foliage creates the framework of a garden. It acts as a foil for flowers and helps link together the various colors. In its own right it forms a decorative element, exhibiting many colors, textures, and shapes. These hostas easily demonstrate this, beautifully setting off the hardy geranium as well as contributing color and interesting shapes to the scene.

small trees and shrubs

Structure
Structure, provided by trees and shrubs, is an important element in the garden, especially during winter, when herbaceous plants have died back below ground. It is also of great significance during the summer months. As other plants come and go, structure adds a sense of continuity. Evergreens, such as hollies, box, and conifers, in particular, add a touch of permanence to a garden.

Most trees and shrubs have a limited flowering period, and it is the foliage that provides most of the interest. Some shrubs can be uninteresting when not in flower and have a hard time justifying their presence in a small garden. Choose shrubs that have a good shape and plenty of good foliage, and possibly even autumn color or berries to get the maximum from them. Many trees and shrubs, evergreens in particular, add much to a small garden and need very little in the way of attention.

Small is beautiful
Choose only small trees for a small garden. It is true that by the time trees are big, the planter will not be around to worry about them and somebody will have to take them down. Small trees are more in scale with the smaller garden, and since there are so many to choose from, there is no need to go for such trees as giant oaks.

Autumn color
To get the most out of your trees and shrubs, look closely at what they offer and go for those that suit your needs. Autumn foliage is particularly desirable; the flaming reds and oranges are unbeatable as garden decoration.

Pruning for better foliage
There are a number of trees and shrubs that, if pruned, produce larger and better-colored foliage. Most require cutting back almost to the ground in the spring. Choose a place just above a bud to make the diagonal cut. Several of the elders (Sambucus) respond very well to this, as does Rosa glauca. Eucalyptus gunnii is too big for a small garden when fully grown, but it can be pruned to not only keep it much smaller but also to produce better foliage.

▶ ▶ Also see: Seasonal plants and shrubs, pages 38–39

Topiary

Although it is the underlying structure of branches and twigs that gives a tree or bush its shape, it is the foliage that fills it out and turns it into a solid object. This is important where trees are used as silhouettes, as in the case of tall conifers, for example, but it is even more important where the tree or shrub has been specifically shaped as it is in topiary. Simple geometric shapes such as balls, cubes, and cones can be created directly from the shrub by cutting the branches to shape as they grow. More complicated shapes need to have a wooden or metal armature inside to which branches are trained and the outline sculpted as the shrub grows. Topiary is not difficult, but patience is required; box and yew are slow growing.

Small trees

Acer griseum
Acer japonicum
Acer pseudoplatanus 'Brilliantissima'
Amelanchier lamarckii
Betula pendula 'Youngii'
Cercis siliquastrum
Cornus
Crataegus
Gleditsia triacanthos 'Sunburst'
Ilex
Laburnum watereri 'Vossii'
Magnolia stellata
Malus 'Profusion'
Malus sargentii
Prunus serrula
Prunus subhirtella 'Autumnalis'
Pyrus salicifolia 'Pendula'
Rhus typhina
Sorbus
Syringa

Suitable shrubs for topiary

Buxus sempervirens
Ilex
Laurus nobilis
Ligustrum ovalifolium
Taxus baccata

Evergreens

Evergreen trees and shrubs are excellent for providing structure and interest in a garden year-round. While a few conifers, such as Leyland cypress, are very fast-growing, many are extremely slow-growing and are therefore ideal for the small garden. Most evergreens, including conifers, need virtually no pruning or other attention. However, many evergreens, especially conifers, can become a little dull, so mix them with other shrubs.

Easy maintenance
An evergreen border (above) not only provides year-round interest but also provides a border that needs little maintenance. The shrubs need little pruning and their thick foliage creates a perfect ground cover to keep the weeds down. Tight-growing evergreens, such as box (left) and yew are ideal subjects for creating topiary. Simple geometric shapes such as these spheres can be clipped without the need for internal formers.

retirement remedies

Carry on gardening

Not all gardeners are active. Some are elderly and less able than they once were, while others have a disability that prevents them from gardening in the conventional manner. Gardening is great for people with physical limitations. It not only supplies an interest, but it also offers gentle exercise as well as the opportunity to get outside and do something other than simply sitting in the sun. Fortunately, there are ways for people to continue to garden in one form or another, including creating miniature gardens in seed trays.

Safety and comfort

Safety measures must be taken before someone with limited abilities begins gardening. Surfaces should not be slippery, and glass and water should be kept away from places where people move about. Once the problem of moving around the garden has been resolved, there is the question of what jobs can be comfortably carried out. As will be seen over the next few pages, there is a surprising amount. Some people will be able to garden in the conventional manner, with the exception that some tools will have to be adapted to make them more easily held. Others will need to have the garden brought up to them so that it can be attended from a sitting or standing position.

Scaling it down

One of the secrets of limited gardening is to acknowledge one's limitations and scale down the garden accordingly. Things like mowing lawns and digging may be too strenuous, whereas tending a few raised beds with nothing more than a hand fork and trowel may well be possible. For others, it may be necessary to scale down even further and create a miniature garden in a container that may be placed on a table or even a lap.

Plants to use

Plants that are prickly or difficult to handle are best avoided, as well as those that form large and cumbersome clumps. The partially sighted will enjoy colors that stand out and are likely to have a preference for powerful scents.

Easy harvesting
Climbing ladders is an occupation that few elderly or less able gardeners can undertake. Fortunately, fruit growers have bred fruit trees of all types that can be easily picked from ground level, omitting the need to climb or even stretch. It is worth searching these trees out and planting one or two as there is nothing quite like freshly picked fruit. In many cases the trees can be grown against walls or wire framework, but there are an increasing number of varieties that can be grown in containers, which is handy for people in wheelchairs.

Under cover

The weather is not always kind to gardeners and the elderly may have difficulty scurrying for cover, so it is a good idea to provide easily accessible shelter from sudden downpours. Similarly, they may not want to be in the sun all the time, so shady places should be available, both for relaxing and for working with pots. During inclement weather, working in a greenhouse can be a pleasant occupation. Alternatively, a conservatory attached to the house may be adapted as a greenhouse, providing the opportunity for year-round gardening.

Gardening for the blind

There are many partially sighted and even blind gardeners. One of their keys to success is to be able to find their way around. The garden should be well laid out in a logical design and the different areas should be well flagged so that gardeners can easily find their own way around. Many of the tools visually impaired gardeners use are conventional, but tools such as measuring sticks should be marked with indentations.

design and surfaces

Care must be taken with the design of the garden for the elderly and those with restricted abilities. Difficult corners, steps, and slippery surfaces should be eliminated and flower beds should be designed so they are accessible and easy to reach, even from a wheelchair, if needed.

Paths

One of the most important aspects of designing a garden for the elderly or disabled is to make certain that access is easy and safe. Paths should be wide enough for a person with a cane or a wheelchair to pass freely along. The surface should be free from bumps or any edges that may cause a person to trip, but they should not be so smooth that they are slippery. A textured surface will allow a grip as well as prevent glare, which may temporary dazzle or even blind people if they are looking at the ground as they walk. Brick paths are notorious for attracting very slippery algae and moss and should therefore either be replaced or regularly treated with an algicide. Wooden surfaces also can be very slippery when wet and should be avoided unless it is possible to improve the grip on them by cutting ridges into the surface. Attaching chicken wire is very effective, but it is only really suitable for wheelchairs, as the elderly could stumble if their shoes catch on the very rough surface.

Safe paths
As people get older, their risk of slipping or tripping increases. Make certain that all paths are free from sudden unevenness. Paths should, however, have a roughened surface to discourage slipping. The garden area should be well-drained so that there is no standing water or puddles. Using contrasting colors along the edge of gardens or lawns will help to delineate the paths for the partially sighted. Avoid unnecessary curves or corners.

▶ ▶ Also see: Pathways, pages 94–95, Steps and stairways, pages 106–107

Stepping out
If possible, replace steps with a gently sloping ramp, or at least provide a ramp as an alternative. All steps should be flanked by sturdy handrails. Handrails can also be used along the edge of terraces or difficult paths. It is important that the rails inspire confidence; they should be well fixed and not rock about or move. Wooden handrails should be regularly inspected to make certain that they have not rotted and are not likely to collapse suddenly.

Steps

Steps should be eliminated if possible and replaced by a gentle slope. Even elderly persons who are not infirm will find pushing wheelbarrows or mowing machines up steps to be an increasingly difficult task. Slopes, or any other tricky areas, should be lined with handrails.

Access

Pathways should also be wide enough for wheelchairs and people with canes. This applies not only to gateways and archways, but also greenhouse doorways and other buildings. Handles on doors and gates should be easy to reach and use.

Glass

Glass is potentially dangerous. Inside greenhouses, the gardener is kept away from the glass by the staging, but you might have to put protection near the doors. Avoid putting paths alongside a greenhouse where someone might fall and hit the building. A fence alongside the greenhouse can help. Similarly, avoid using cold frames with glass lights. Use plastic or even polyethylene which is much safer than glass, although not quite as effective.

gardening made easy

Gardening for the elderly or disabled is not only about safety, it is also about ways and means of looking after plants. One of the biggest problems is that the ground is a long way down for somebody who cannot easily bend or kneel. The solution is to bring the ground closer in one way or another.

Reaching out
The elderly often have difficulty gripping conventional tools. Life is made considerably easier by buying special tools with handles that have been adapted for easy use (right). Being able to perform work that involves reaching is another problem and, again, special tools can help. They can be purchased or made with extended handles (above) so that the user does not have to bend.

Tools

The right tools are essential for the elderly and disabled. Tools need not be expensive or complicated. For example, a length of plastic water pipe provides a simple way to sow seed from a wheelchair. Some people may like to make their own, but there is an increasing number of tools available from specialist shops.

There are two important aspects to choosing tools: select tools with long handles and an easy grip. Long handles prevent the need for bending or leaning forward. Many people have increasing difficulty gripping normal handles and need special handles that are easier to hold.

Cutting out the difficult jobs

Attending plants is not too arduous, but things like mowing the lawn and cutting hedges become more difficult as the years pass. Sad as it is to see the lawn go, it may be time to consider altering the garden so that the lawn is turned over to a paved area or perhaps to shrubs or ground-cover plants. Similarly, unless you can help cut hedges, a fence or wall becomes an easier proposition. With foresight, you can give yourself an easy-care garden for your later years. A yew hedge, for example, planted well ahead of your old age, will be easier to tend as it only needs cutting once a year.

Raised beds

Another way of making life easier is to bring the soil up to workable height. This involves some form of raised bed. The height and shape may vary depending on the person using it. Work from wheelchairs, for example, is much easier if the bed is raised as this eliminates any bending. The wheelchair can be brought alongside or even pushed up tight against the side of the bed if there is a knee hole or overhang all the way around. The raised beds can be built from brick or stone, or they can be purchased in plastic. Ordinary chairs or stools can also be used with raised beds.

Within reach
Bringing the soil up to a workable height is one solution for those who have difficulty bending. Raised beds (left) make tending plants much easier. It is possible to make special "T"-shaped beds so that a wheelchair can be maneuvered under the top (like a table), bringing the work surface even closer. Fruit trees and shrubs (below) should be limited in height to provide easy access.

Overreaching

Bending is a problem for many gardeners, but reaching above the head or into the distance is also difficult. Fruit trees, for example, can become impossible to climb or reach. The need to reach forward can be eliminated by using narrow borders. Use fruit trees that grow at the right height for attending from a standing position or from a wheelchair.

entrances and exits

Making an entrance

Usually, a garden already has an entrance when a house is purchased, and many people, therefore, do not give it a second thought. However, it pays to look carefully at both the entrance to the house and garden, and also to the various entrances and exits between different areas of the garden.

First and last

The entrance to a garden is one of the most important features as it sets the tone for the rest of the garden. It invariably provides the first impression that visitors will have of the garden. Similarly, the exit is the last thing seen by visitors, and it leaves a lasting impression.

Setting the tone

The type of entrance and the way that it is executed sets the tone of the garden. It should be in keeping with the style of the garden. For example, a formal garden needs a formal entrance, while a cottage garden can have a much more relaxed approach.

Keeping the world at bay

One must not forget that an entrance to a garden was traditionally the guardian of one's safety. It was there to allow entrance through the defenses that kept out animals and foe. While it is not usually quite so heavily fortified now, the garden entrance still performs that basic function: it shuts out the outside world. This does not mean that entrances should be threatening, but they are best if they look strong enough to be closed, even if they never are.

Beyond the threshold

Nowadays, the barriers around a garden are used more for privacy than for the purpose of supplying a physical barricade. The entrance usually is the one place a person can see into the garden. The gateway, therefore, is not only a physical entrance to a garden but also a visual one. As you enter, you have a glimpse of what lies beyond. In a well-executed garden, this glimpse is tantalizing—it draws you in.

Just looking

As with so many aspects of garden design, it is good to simply stand and stare at the aspect you are evaluating. Stand outside any external or internal entrance and just look through it. Note whether it is enticing and whether it is representative of what lies beyond. Does the entrance reveal too much or too little? How can it be improved? Does the type of path and its condition make the right statement? Does it need changing or improving?

Improving the view

When evaluating your garden from its entry points, ask yourself if the view itself needs enhancing in any way. Perhaps a focal point should be added to draw the eye. Maybe the direction of the path should be altered so that it moves enticingly out of view. If the gateway directs the eye to the entrance of the house, does anything need to be done to improve the area around the door, or even the door itself?

Getting inspiration

Because the main entrance is usually on the road, it is possible to see plenty of examples and collect ideas simply by walking around a neighborhood. The exercise is a good one as you will see bad examples as well as good ones. You will become aware of the pitfalls and so be able to avoid things that either do not work or are out of keeping with what you want to create.

Picture-perfect
A gateway can be a dramatic introduction to a garden. The archway serves several functions beside the obvious one of holding the gate up. As can be seen here, archways act as a support for climbing plants such as roses, clematis, and honeysuckle. They also frame the garden beyond, frequently creating an enticing image, and drawing the visitor through to investigate.

driveways

Drive-in
Driveways are large and difficult to disguise. However, it is possible to make them so that they are attractive as well as practical. They should be wide enough that people do not have to stand on the borders when getting out of cars and, if possible, they should have an interesting curving shape (right). You can soften the edges with shrubs and other plants.
If the drive is a straight one with two strips of concrete or slabs (opposite), place low-growing plants along the middle.

Driveways are one of the most difficult things to incorporate into a garden. Unless they are grand, elegantly sweeping to the front of a mansion, they are not particularly beautiful. This is because they are purely functional. They are used as somewhere to park the car, somewhere to load or get into the car, or as access to the garage. Frequently, they have even less attractive qualities, such as being somewhere to dump a load of sand or bricks, or somewhere to store a camper or a boat. However, there are many ways to improve the appearance of a driveway.

The base
A driveway must be well built as it bears a heavy load. A driveway that sags or has a broken surface is not only an eyesore but is also potentially dangerous. If you have to construct your own and have any doubts about your abilities, have it built professionally. It must have a solid foundation of rammed hardcore topped with a layer of concrete and finished with whatever surface you want.

The surface
Concrete is the best foundation. It should be sprayed with tar and a layer of gravel should be rolled into it. A thin, loose layer can be laid on top to get the noise and characteristic wheel marks. A concrete surface can be left as the final finish. This will look raw for some time, but it will eventually tone down. It is the best surface to have`if

you intend to receive payloads of sand, or for mixing concrete on; these activities would spoil any other surface.

Tarmac has a rather industrial appearance, but once it weathers it has a certain softness to its look. Normally it is black turning to grey, but it can be obtained in other colors and can have white chips rolled in to relieve the surface.

Gravel drives are very attractive both to the eye and to the ear as they produce a satisfying crunch under the wheels of a car. They should have a solid foundation and should not be laid directly on the soil.

Brick or pavers are increasingly being used for drives. They produce an attractive, decorative surface. They must have a good surface under them.

Paving slabs can be used but, again, they should be on a concrete base to

prevent unevenness. Various colors and patterns are available.

Welcoming scents
It is difficult to disguise a driveway. It can be edged with shrubs so that it is not visible from the rest of the garden, but for security reasons, this might not be desirable. Herbaceous plants can be an attractive alternative. If possible, position a fragrant shrub or plant near the area where you stop the car as this will be a most welcome smell after a day's work and, with luck, will remove some of the tensions of the outside world.

Making use of plants
An old-fashioned way of creating a drive that is not so overpowering as the all-over modern method, is to lay two strips of concrete where the wheels are to run. This leaves a rather awkward strip of earth down the middle, which can be left to grass, or it can be used for low, flowering plants. There are a number of attractive low-growing plants that are too much like thugs to put in open borders, where they overtake everything. Containment between the concrete strips is ideal for these plants as they fight it out among themselves without interfering with more delicate plants. Acaena, pratia, elder, and thyme are four such plants.

gates and porches

Suit the situation
Try and fit the gateway or porch to the style of garden or building. Both the gate (right) and the porch (far right) are rustic to suit their cottage-like situation. Choice of the right style and its interpretation is very important as gateways and porches are two things that visitors first notice, and they set the tone for what is to come.

Internal gateways
Although a heavy metal gate with solid brick piers (opposite) gives the impression of impregnable security, it also acts as a welcoming entrance. It frames the view beyond and makes the visitor want to pass through to see what lies there. Even internal gateways, where security is not of prime concern, can be of a heavy construction, to an advantage.

The visual impact of both gateways and porches is enormous. A great deal of thought needs to be put into what they should look like and how they can be made, even if someone else is employed to make them.

Simple gateways

The simplest of gateways is just a hole in a hedge or fence. While this can work well for internal boundaries it is not very satisfactory for external boundaries. Next to this a wooden or metal gate without any frills is inserted into the fence or hedge.

There is a great range of gates available, some simple, others very ornate. Normally, the gate is the same height as the fence, or smaller if the "fence" is a high hedge. Make certain that the bases of the gateposts are buried deeply into the ground (at least 30 inches) and held firmly with concrete.

Archways

A more complicated but more interesting way of creating a gateway is to introduce an arch. The archway can be a simple framework built from wood or metal, or it can be a solid object created from brick or by letting a hedge grow up and over the gate. Gates in arches can be more complicated in design and are often tall.

Porches

Porches are more of an architectural feature than a garden feature. They are often no more than a simple framework with climbers growing over them. Porches can be of similar construction to arches in other parts of the garden, except that one side is attached to a building. Make certain that the porch is big enough if climbers are to be used, as they will hang through the framework, restricting the size of the entrance and may possibly scratch people entering if the structure is too small. Never add a porch that is out of keeping with the building.

Climbers

Apart from those constructed from hedging, arches over gateways are perfect for growing climbing plants. Roses are ideal, but thornless varieties should be chosen, if possible. Clematis make good companions to roses, and between them, you will have a long period of flowering.

pathways

On the road

Paths are an important aspect of garden design and should always be thought about very carefully. They not only provide the means of getting from one place to another with dry feet, but they also have a strong visual importance. There is a wide range of materials to suit all situations and tastes.

Visual importance

On entering a new area of garden the viewer automatically looks along the course of the path as it winds through borders, shrubs, and other features. This has two implications. The first is that paths are always noticed and should therefore be well designed and constructed, using sympathetic materials. The second is that the path must lead somewhere visually as well as physically. It must lead to a focal point, a piece of sculpture or a specimen plant perhaps, or it should drift out of view around a corner, giving a sense of mystery and implying that there is more to come.

Straight paths

Plan carefully where to place a path. A path down the middle of the garden dissects it into two halves. This may be convenient if you want rows of vegetables on either side, but it does very little from the aesthetic point of view. It is also impractical if you have a lawn spanning the garden as it will be split in two by the path. A path down one side has a practical ring to it; however, it leaves a lot of the garden without direct access to either see or tend what is there. Straight paths tend to be dull unless skillfully handled (a pergola or a series of arches will transform one). Do keep in mind, though, if a path is used a great deal, a straight one is the most convenient.

Meandering paths

Paths that wander around a garden tend to promote a leisurely wander; straight paths tend to draw the visitor through as quickly as possible. Paths that wind their way between borders give the feeling of being right in the midst of the plants, which allows one to feel much more involved with their growth.

Shortcuts

Human beings are prone to take the shortest route from A to B. Therefore, in certain circumstances it is often good to avoid sharp angles in a path, particularly if there is not a fence or building within the angle. Inevitably people will take a shortcut across the angle even if there is a bed or border there. This is particularly true in the case of front gardens, where regular visitors such as newspaper carriers and letter carriers always (quite naturally) try to reduce the amount of distance involved at each house. Make front paths as direct as possible from the front gate to the door. Any paths leading from it that are used purely to wander around the garden can be as convoluted as you like.

Materials

There is a wide choice of materials for use as garden paths. For much-used paths, a hard surface, such as paving slabs, is preferred. Paths that are used mainly for wandering along in summer can be made of less durable material. Grass is one of the cheapest and the easiest options, although it will frequently have to be mowed and it can become muddy and worn in a wet climate. Gravel is softer than slabs of stone or concrete, but it is more weatherproof and durable than grass. It also looks very good and makes a satisfying crunch when walked upon. The cheapest of all is a simple beaten-earth path, as was commonly used in many old-fashioned cottages.

The way ahead
Pathways are an extremely important part of any garden. They are visual arteries as well as physical ones; they carry the eye as well as the feet. The nature and quality of a path should never be skimped on. They can be made from a wide number of materials. Paving slabs, pictured here, are one of the easiest methods for achieving good results.

brick and stone

Brick
Although man-ufactured, brick is a natural material. The color is usually based on earth colors, which work well in a garden situation where it blends with soil and plants. Brick is very versatile and lends itself to the imagin-ation as it can be used to create all manner of shapes and patterns.

Brick makes an excellent pathway. One of the most durable materials is red brick or those made from some sort of stone, such as concrete. Brick is a hard material both physically and visually, and needs to be handled carefully in a garden so that it complements the overall design. Plan carefully, as a good path will last a long time.

Brick
Brick paths are among the most beautiful, and can be laid in a number of traditional patterns. But it is important to get the color and pattern right and to be sure that they are frost-proof. Special pavers can be used, but these are usually more uniform than bricks and do not produce the same feel. Bricks can be laid on a concrete foundation, or, if the path is not too heavily used, they can be laid on rammed hardcore blinded with sand.

Bricks can be slippery if used in a damp or shady place, and should be scrubbed or treated with an algicide to keep them safe.

Paving slabs
Although they may not always look particularly elegant, paving slabs are very practical. The larger sizes are big enough to be laid onto rammed earth without necessarily laying a concrete foundation as long as there is not too much heavy traffic. Another advantage is that they can be lifted and reused, making it easy to redesign the garden.

Genuine stone slabs are very expensive, but there are some good reproduction ones which have a textured surface. If you make your own, it helps if the concrete is brushed over before it sets hard to remove some of the cement and to expose some of the small stones. This leaves an attractive texture.

Natural colored slabs tend to look best in paths; colored ones often clash with the plants in the borders.

▶ ▶ Also see: Surfaces, pages 10–11, Steps and stairways, pages 106–107

Crazy paving

Pieces of irregular paving or stones can be used to create a path with an informal, almost haphazard, look. Such paths feel friendly and are particularly good in cottage-style and other informal gardens. Match the stones well so that the gaps are not too large; otherwise there will be large areas of cement showing. The edge can be irregular, as here, or lined with brick to finish it more neatly. Plants pouring over the edges make it look even more informal.

Mixed media

Paving slabs can look bleak at times. Mixing them with other materials makes a difference in their appearance. A row of bricks on either side, with the occasional transverse one, lifts the look of the slabs completely. Mixing plain concrete slabs with some that are surfaced with large pebbles also makes an interesting contrast.

Crazy paving

Crazy paving can be made from broken slabs of paving of varying sizes. This kind of paving requires a firm base, either rammed hardcore topped with sand or a layer of concrete. Mixed colors can be effective if used well, particularly in designs for a Mediterranean type of garden, but plain slabs tend to draw less attention to themselves.

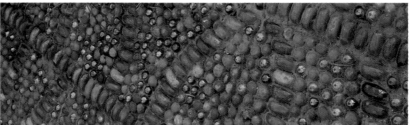

Cobblestone

Granite sets are expensive, but they produce a beautiful path. A mass of them may be overpowering, so mixing them with another medium, such as gravel or slabs is ideal. Keep in mind that because they are uneven they can be a little uncomfortable to walk on. Large, rounded pebbles can be used in the same way, but these are decidedly uncomfortable if you have to walk a long way. Pebble paths are best used for short distances or for decoration.

Concrete

Concrete makes a solid, practical path. Initially, the fresh concrete has a raw appearance, but this will eventually weather to a much softer appearance, which can look quite attractive. One disadvantage is that a lot of effort is needed to lift and relay fresh concrete, should you decide to move the path. A foundation of rammed hardcore is needed for a concrete path.

earth, wood, and gravel

Earth, grass, and gravel are much softer materials for paths than stone or brick both to walk on and to look at. They are also, generally, cheaper options. Softer materials have an advantage over harder options in that they can be more easily relaid in another direction or position.

Earthen paths

Earthen paths are just that: earth. They are beaten hard and kept clear of weeds by the constant passage of feet. They are the traditional paths of cottage gardens and were very often supplemented by the addition of ash from the fire and occasional stones thrown out of the surrounding flower and vegetable beds. Over time, these materials form a hard crust that prevents the path from becoming muddy in wet weather. They are best for old-fashioned-style gardens or in more formal situations, for paths that are tucked away from sight.

Grass paths

Grass paths are cheap to produce and are generally very good to look at. But they suffer from one big drawback: they require mowing at frequent intervals. Unfortunately, a shaggy path can make the whole garden look untidy even if it is not. If you do not have time to mow the grass, at least clip the edges. It makes a surprising difference. Avoid using grass paths were there is heavy activity, as the grass will wear thin in places. If necessary, use a heavy-duty grass that can withstand trampling. Use a good-quality grass or grass seed and make certain that all perennial weeds have been removed from the soil before planting or laying seed. Any weeds in the lawn will constantly try to spread into the borders, involving a lot of unnecessary work to remove them.

Wandering off
Loose material, such as gravel or small stones, make an ideal path as they are dry and yet soft to walk on. Many make a crunching sound under the shoes, which is not only pleasantly satisfying but can also act as an early security warning. Gravel paths work best if they have some form of edging to prevent the stones from working their way into the borders.

Gravel

Gravel has much to offer despite its probably being the most expensive of the three options. It generally looks very attractive, especially after it has just been raked. Depending on the color—and different areas of origin provide gravels of different colors—the path will set off the flowers and other plants well. Maintenance consists

▶ ▶ Also see: Garden floors pages, 108–109, Surfaces, pages 110–111

Softly, softly
Left: Chipped bark
is one of the easiest
and most instant
paths to lay; just tip
it from a bag. It is
very soft underfoot.
However, it is very
informal looking
and is best used in
this style of garden
It is probably most
at home on paths
through trees and
shrubs where it
creates a natural
woodland feel.

Green paths
Far left: Grass is
possibly the most
natural of materials
for paths as it is
composed of living
material. It has the
disadvantage of
needing to be cut
and is not very good
in wet weather and
winter. Also, it can
wear under heavy
use. Having said that,
it is very difficult to
beat in terms of
appearance, espec-
ially when the path
continues on
naturally from a
lawn or other
grassy area.

of treating with weed killer or weeding
by hand and raking the path over. If the
gravel has been laid on compacted
earth, it is inevitable that some will
work its way down into the soil and it
will be necessary to add a few bags of
fresh gravel every so often. If possible,
line the edge of the path with a curb
or other edging so that the gravel does
not wander into borders.

Wood chippings
Wood chips are becoming increasingly
available. These make marvelous soft
paths, especially through shrubs and
trees. Lay the bark on compacted soil
between lines of logs or wood edging.
Over time, the chips will decompose,
so it is necessary to replenish them
when their cover wears thin.

stepping stones

Stepping out
For areas that only take light traffic, stepping stones can be ideal. They are practical in that they help keep the feet dry and yet at the same time they are visually exciting. Children love them. Any shape of stone can be used, either regular or irregular. Rounds of tree trunk can also be used (far right), but they can become slippery in wet weather, especially in shady positions.

Paths are not always the appropriate solution for creating access. A solid path across a lawn or through a border, for example, might create too strong a visual line. Replacing it with a broken line of a series of stepping stones may well be the solution. Stepping stones can also be used where access is limited. For example, a series of stones could be used to provide a firm surface for anyone working in a flower border, while visitors would be inclined to keep to the clearly defined main paths.

Stone stones
Depending on the circumstances, stepping stones can either be regular or irregular in shape. In a formal garden, round or square stones or slabs provide the best appearance, but stones randomly placed, such as those used to provide limited access to a flower bed, are better arranged in an irregular outline. If the stones extend into grass, they should be sunk a little lower than the surface of the lawn so that the grass can be mown without hitting the stone.

Stone on stones
Grass and borders are not the only places to use stepping stones. They can look extremely attractive crossing a large area of gravel, or even sunk into an area of concrete to create a contrasting pattern.

Walking on water
In the ground, stepping stones are more likely to be slabs rather than actual stones, but for use in water across a small pond or stream, they should be three-dimensional stones. These can look very attractive, however, they must be firmly planted and not move. Be careful how you place the stone if the pond has a plastic or rubber liner, as the stone may puncture it.

Wooden stones
An attractive alternative to stone stepping stones is wood. The most usual form this takes is with pieces cut from a felled tree trunk. These are sunk into the ground in exactly the same way as stones. They look most appealing in areas where there are trees and shrubs. Because they are in contact with damp earth they can rot easily, so it is a good idea to treat them with a preservative before laying them. Wood can be very slippery in wet weather or in a damp position. If they are likely to be used in these conditions, nail some chicken wire over the surface; it will make the wood grip-fast without spoiling its appearance.

▶ ▶ Also see: Pathways, pages 94–95; Brick and stone, pages 96–97

Walking on water
Real stepping stones over the base of a pond or stream are always fun. They should be stable and not too rounded or there is the risk of slipping, even if the water is only ankle deep. Be careful if there are young children around as stepping stones over water will draw them like a magnet, with possible unfortunate consequences.

slopes

On level ground

Some gardeners regard a sloping garden as a nuisance, and others welcome one as a blessing. The reluctance to accept a sloping garden is usually because the gardener cannot face the initial amount of work and cost required to turn the slope into an advantage. From a design standpoint, having a plot on several levels is a wonderful opportunity to create an interesting garden.

Flattening the garden

One solution would be to flatten the whole garden, lowering one end and raising the other. The main advantage of a flat garden would be if the gardener were elderly or disabled and had difficulty with steps and slopes. Many vegetable gardeners would prefer a flat surface on which to work, but some of the best vegetable producers live on the sides of mountains, creating terraces in which to grow their produce. Unless infirmity necessitates a flat garden, go with it and utilize the slopes.

Slopes or terraces

One of the best ways of dealing with a slope is to flatten it out in sections or terraces so that there are level areas for beds, lawns, and places to sit. These level places are interconnected with sloping paths and steps. There is no reason why the garden should not simply be left as a slope and gardened as if it were flat. This method easily works if the slope is only a minor one; if it begins to get steep, the loose top soil will gradually work its way down the slope. Another disadvantage of a steep slope is that it is very tiring to work on it.

Holding back the slope

If the slope is flattened into a series of terraces, there must be a way of holding back the soil to prevent it all from moving down the hill. The simplest way is to alter the garden from one continuous slope to a series of flat areas supported by much steeper slopes or banks. This, in effect, is recontouring the slope. Another, usually more attractive, way is to build a series of retaining walls. These can be left plain or used as a home for rock-loving plants.

Using contours

Not all slopes are one-directional; they often move in different directions, or there may be promontories sticking out. Make use of these to contour the slope. It will look much more interesting than a series of parallel slopes.

Decking

One way of dealing with a slope without having to move much earth is to use wooden decking built to extend over the slope. Hardwood is by far the best material, but soft wood can be used as long as it is treated with a wood preservative and is well prepared to prevent splinters. Decking can be a perfect place for entertaining and relaxing

Creating a slope

There is no reason why terraces should not be created in a flat garden; it always adds interest. One way to do this is to build a patio that is raised above the surrounding garden. An alternative is to do the opposite and excavate a sitting area that is lower than the surrounding beds. It need not be deep; even 6 inches will be enough to emphasize the different areas. Another way of creating a variety of heights in the garden is to build a rock garden or an artificial slope with a small stream running down it.

Flowers in the bank
A bank of flowering plants is more likely to make a strong visual impact than the same flowers planted on flat ground. A garden on a slope can be much more interesting than a flat one, but it can also be very tiring for the elderly, especially when mowing or moving wheelbarrows.

terraces and retaining walls

Terraces may conjure up images of gardens clinging to the side of mountains, but even a modest slope can be terraced. Basically, it simply means flattening out certain areas of a slope using banks or retaining walls to compensate for the slope. A lot of effort may be involved, but the rewards are tremendous.

A bank or a wall

Banks are cheaper and easier to construct than walls. In an informal design they work perfectly, although low ones are usually visually better and physically more stable than taller ones. Retaining walls are generally much more attractive and will fit in with most styles of garden. If planting holes are left in the brick or stone work, they can be decorated with plants.

Building walls

Retaining walls may be holding back a great deal of weight. If a gardener has any doubt about his or her abilities to construct one, then it is safer to enlist the help of a professional builder. A low wall that is more decorative rather than supportive is well within the capabilities of most gardeners. Carefully work out the levels and redistribute the soil. Be careful not to mix up the topsoil and the subsoil; retaining walls will need good foundations. The wall itself can be built from stone, brick, or concrete blocks, the last not being particularly attractive, but probably the cheapest. Slope the wall back slightly towards the terrace.

Drainage

Water may build up behind the wall so drainage pipes should be inserted at intervals. Alternatively, the vertical pointing between bricks or stones can be left out every so often. The drainage outlets should be at ground level on the lower slope side. Before filling in the gap between the wall and the slope, pour in a layer of rubble to help with the drainage. Ideally, this should go right along the wall level with the drainage holes, but if there is not enough space, a quantity around each hole will suffice.

Retaining walls
The expression "retaining wall" can conjure up a bleak image of the reinforced concrete used in civil engineering projects. However, in the garden, retaining walls can be treated much more sympathetically, as these two contrasting images illustrate. As well as leveling the ground, a retaining wall offers the opportunity for a decorative element that fits in with the style of the garden.

▶ ▶ Also see: Outer boundaries, pages 118–119

Backfilling

The retaining wall should be built a little way from the terrace so that there is work access for both sides. Once it is complete, this gap should be filled in with soil to complete the terrace. Make certain that the top layer is topsoil. If you intend to plant along the top of the wall, it does no harm to fill the entire gap with topsoil.

Planting

Some retaining walls, especially dry stone walling, look splendid with a few plants growing over them. There are normally enough gaps in a dry stone wall to push in some compost and a plant, but gaps must be left in a cemented stone or brick wall. Be certain that the gaps do not weaken the wall. It is sometimes possible to squash the root ball of a plant and then slide it in. It is often easier to start from scratch by blowing seed into a crevice or easing a rooted cutting (roots wrapped in dampened tissue paper), along with some compost, into a crevice.

Plants for walls

Aubrieta
Aurinia saxatilis
Armeria juniperifolia
Campanula portenschlagiana
Erigeron karvinskianus
Lewisia cotyledon
Phlox douglasii
Phlox subulata

Retaining steps

Steps can be built directly into a slope, but can look clumsy if allowed simply to disappear into the earth on either side. A stepped retaining wall makes a much better finish. It can also be used for holding the plants back, preventing them from over-growing the steps in a way that might become dangerous.

steps and stairways

Rustic steps
Rustic steps (right and center) have a wonderfully romantic appeal about them. In spite of their casual appearance they should be well constructed and safely bedded into the ground. They are probably best for little-used byways than as regular paths, as they can become dangerous in wet weather and during winter.

Access between different levels is extremely important. For example, at the entrance to a garden, steps tend to attract the eye and invite the visitor to ascend, particularly if the top is hidden from sight by a stunning array of plants. There is a wide range of materials and styles, ranging from the formal to the informal.

Styles

Steps can be built into a bank, or they can be built freestanding, in front of a bank. Freestanding steps are really best suited to formal gardens, but they may be suitable for other gardens if a retaining wall is already in existence, as it is far less trouble to build the steps in front than it is to cut through the wall to the bank. Straight stairways have a formality about them; but those curving away into the undergrowth are far less formal.

Materials

Bricks are attractive and adaptable and can be used for a range of styles. Stone is very attractive and is particularly suitable in areas where it is the local building material. Stone steps may be formal or informal. Concrete blocks are not very attractive, but they are easy to use. Paving slabs are very easy to use and they are relatively cheap; plain ones may look a bit uninteresting. Wood is very attractive, but may become very slippery; chicken wire nailed to the surface will make them nonslip. Logs and sleepers (railway ties) can be used for the risers on a staircase where the steps are filled with gravel, small stones, or bark. This method is inexpensive and very attractive for an informal setting.

▶ ▶ Also see: Garden floors, pages 108–109; Entrances and exits, pages 88–89

Plantings for steps

The angularity of steps and stairways can be softened by growing plants on them. While this is a good idea and has a lot to recommend it, safety must be the first consideration. Do not do anything that could cause people to trip or slip. Plants, such as ivy, for example, can be grown along the risers of the steps and clipped back out of harm's way. Softer plants, such as *Erigeron karvinskianus,* can be used in cracks and crevices. Other plants can be allowed to encroach over the sides of steps, as long as they do not cover the steps completely or are dangerous in any way.

Handrails

Handrails can look unattractive but they may be necessary if elderly people are likely to visit the garden. With care, they can be made to fit in with the style of the steps and not be too obtrusive.

Ramps and slopes

It is sensible to include a few slopes in a garden's overall design. These will not only be welcomed by those who have difficulties with steps, but also by the gardener when it comes to moving wheelbarrows and lawnmowers about.

Joint ownership
Steps can be softened and given greater appeal if they are partially overgrown with plants (above and center). However, make certain that there is enough tread so they are safe to use. Steps that wind away to disappear through a haze of plants immediately excite the sense of adventure and draw the visitor upwards.

garden floors

Ground cover

One tends to think of a garden as simply being covered in soil, but a great deal of the soil is likely to be hidden beneath some form of covering. Variation in surfaces makes the garden visually more interesting and has practical purposes as well.

Purpose

When considering the design of the garden and the surfaces that will be required, it is important to think about the purpose and uses of the garden. If the sole purpose is to grow plants, then the majority of the garden will reach the borders. If you want areas to sit and relax or entertain in, a mix of paved patios and lawns are required. If there are children around, then play areas will be important. Children may well require hard surfaces to ride or skate on and softer, grassy surfaces for games.

Hard or soft

Garden surfaces are usually hard or soft. Hard surfaces include paving slabs, concrete, and bricks; soft surfaces include grass and wood chips. As a rule of thumb, hard surfaces are expensive to lay but inexpensive and easy to maintain. Softer surfaces, on the other hand, are generally less expensive to lay, but more expensive both in time and maintainance cost.

Patios

Nearly every garden has a terrace or a patio. Generally, these are placed near the house, and often immediately against it. This is convenient for bringing food and drinks outside, and has the advantage of acting as a visual link between the house and the garden. However, if this area is in permanent shade, it may well be better placed elsewhere.

Patios can appear stark and bare, with little character, because of the choice of surface or because they are not softened with plants. Avoid glaring white or pale yellow surfaces that reflect the sun back up into the eyes. Choose a surface that is either textured or a soft, neutral color. Plain concrete is very harsh when first laid, but it weathers down. Paving slabs are probably the cheapest and easiest option, and they are helped visually if they are not laid in serried ranks. Use varying sizes to create a pattern, either formal or random, and perhaps mix the slabs in with other materials, as described below. Patios are usually used a great deal, so make certain that they are laid flat, with just the slightest of slopes to shed rainwater.

Plain or patterned

One advantage of a hard surface is that it is possible to experiment with all kinds of textures and shapes. Paving slabs can be mixed with large pebbles or granite setts. Bricks can be used to create outlines or more solid areas. With imagination, mosaics made from whole or broken tiles can be incorporated. While it may seem to be something that ought to be installed as fast as possible, it is worth spending time looking at examples in books or visiting different public gardens to collect ideas.

Marginal options

Do not forget the edges. Edges are so often overlooked. Patios often look better if they have a low wall around them, or at least a row of contrasting slabs or bricks. Loose material, such as gravel or bark, needs to be retained not only physically but visually, and some form of edging helps enormously. Most lawns even benefit by having a crisp edge (except in informal settings, where they can bleed off under trees and shrubs, although this does lead to mowing difficulties).

Low maintenance
In the ultimate low-maintenance garden, the soil is completely covered and all plants are grown in containers. Here, a paved courtyard covers all available space. When choosing flooring, think of the purpose of the surface, how you will use it, and how much time you will have to maintain it.

surfaces

There are a wide range of materials available to choose from at garden centers and builder's stores and from time to time, unusual materials may come into play. Although cost may be the ultimate deciding factor, try to choose surfaces that are most relevant to your needs and the design of the garden. As a rough rule of thumb, grass goes with plants and hard surfaces with sitting areas and low-maintenance gardens.

Stylish solutions
In country gardens or open areas, grass (right) seems an obvious choice. In town, especially within an enclosed space, another option (opposite) is to use flagstones near the house, complemented by wooden decking covering the rest of the available space.

Paving stones
Paving slabs come in different materials, sizes, and colors. The most expensive is real stone, but there are some good (and bad) reproductions. There are also those made from straightforward concrete. The varying sizes of stones make it possible to produce random or geometric patterns. Some of the colors are a bit garish and should be used with discretion. Natural colors are usually the most aesthetic. Lay the slab on a hardcore base that has been covered with a layer of builder's sand. Bed the stones down well so that they do not move.

Brick
There is a wide selection of brick types available. Avoid those that are not frost-hardy as these will soon crumble. Special bricks for paving (pavers) are widely available, but these are often too regular and produce a rather regimented surface. House bricks are more sympathetic in a garden setting. Earth colors are usually the best choice, but in mixed media surfaces, rich colored ones may blend in well. Bricks are best laid on sand on a concrete base.

Concrete
Used with discretion, this can be an attractive material. Brushing the surface just before it finally sets hard removes some of the cement, exposing the stones in it, for a very attractive finish. Lay it all in one session or the joins and different colors will show. Concrete should be laid on a well-prepared hardcore base.

Grass
Grass is possibly the most natural surface for a garden. It looks good and is sympathetic to the surroundings. With the right choice of grass seed, it can be very hard-wearing. However, grass does have a down side, in that it needs regular mowing, aerating, and treatment to prevent weeds and moss. The ground should be well prepared and all perennial weeds removed or killed before grass is planted. It can be sown or laid with turf, the latter being more expensive but quicker to establish.

Wood chips
Wood chips, or tanbark, provide a soft surface that is particularly suited to children's play areas. It is also a natural-looking surface among trees or shrubs. It is cheaper to buy in bulk if you need a lot (or share with a neighbor) rather than in individual sacks. It can be laid directly onto the surface, or on a layer of perforated horticultural polyethylene, which allows the rainwater to pass through, but stops weeds from coming up.

Gravel
Gravel is an attractive and relatively inexpensive material. It comes in various colors, and the stones can vary in size. Avoid large pebbles, except for detailing, as they are uncomfortable to walk on. Gravel can be laid on compacted soil, or on perforated horticultural polyethylene which prevents weeds from coming up. An edging is advisable to prevent gravel from moving into the borders or lawns. It will need topping up with fresh gravel from time to time, as it works into the soil with use.

Decking
Wooden decking is an attractive surface. It is particularly useful where the ground is uneven or sloping. Depending on the size and scale you want, it might be necessary to have a deck professionally designed, as it can be a formidable structure. If possible, a deck should be built from hardwood.

 ▶ ▶ Also see: Brick and stone, pages 96–97; Earth, wood, and gravel, pages 98–99

disguising essentials

Consider the whole

A garden is a bit like the kitchen or the bathroom in the house: it can be well decorated but it is still a work space and there are bound to be a number of functional bits and pieces around that are not particularly elegant to look at. When designing the garden, all of the space around the house must be considered, even if it is not used for growing plants. You cannot have a pair of garbage cans, for example, standing on the patio and hope no one will see them, just because you may be so used to their presence that you have long since ceased to notice them.

Avoiding the problem

Some objects may go unnoticed because of their familiarity. Think about the appearance of everyday objects such as garbage cans, drains, clotheslines, garden sheds, and garages. Most of the items that will need disguising are likely to be utilitarian. When possible, store items such as garbage cans out of sight. To ensure new garden features do not look out of place, consider design carefully. A garage, for example, can be designed and built in such a way that it is attractive and in no need of disguise. Similarly, garden sheds or greenhouses can be made very attractive in their own right.

Disguise

Many gardeners cannot afford to spend much on a garage, or they have inherited one from the previous owner and cannot afford to replace it. As we will see in the next few pages, there are several ways of hiding objects from view or transforming them into something much more attractive.

Service areas

Sometimes a work area may well be connected with the garden, but it is more of a service area and is better kept out of sight. Rows of plants in pots, for example, or cutting frames and the like in an area devoted to propagation can look messy. The compost bins are rarely an attractive sight, although there is no reason why they should not be designed in such as way that they are.

Concentrate or diversify

Depending on the shape and design of the garden, it might be an idea to concentrate all the eyesores in one spot and cordon off the whole area, or it might be better to scatter them around, with each item disguised and thus less obvious. It may be that one side of the garden needs to be fenced off and used as a storage area. Do not fence things off so well, however, that there is no access. You will need to get to your compost bins with garden waste, and access to a shed should not be so convoluted that it is difficult to get the mower or wheelbarrow out.

Pipe dreams
Drain pipes are not the most attractive of items. Why not hide them and make use of them at the same time? Here a golden hop (Humulus lupulus 'Aureus') is trained up such a pipe. It can be planted directly into the ground or grown in a pot.

Decorating the house

Not all houses are beautiful and in extreme circumstances the appearance of the garden, or the effect that you are trying to create, might be compromised by the house itself. There may not be much that can be done short of rebuilding, but it is surprising what a covering of creepers or climbers will do. The house need not be hidden; colorful window boxes will draw the eye away from the building itself.

hiding utilities

The time and effort spent in disguising items in the garden area is worth it for the overall appearance of the garden. It is possible to hide all types of objects either by construction or gardening, or both. Plants are a natural choice for concealment.

Out of sight
A fence will cover all kinds of eyesores, and plants can be used to make the disguise complete. Plant climbers over fence panels to soften their surface and outline. If it is a shed or garage that is being hidden, then the climbers can be trained directly over its surface using wires or trellising to hold the plants in position.

Fencing it off
The simplest way to hide utilities is to fence off the offending objects. A panel fence will totally hide them from view, but can look as stark as the object it is covering. A fence that allows a partial view through it will not be as severe and will break up the outline of the eyesore to sufficiently disguise it.

Climbing over it
A classic gardener's method of hiding an object is to grow a climbing plant over it. This can be done over the fence or trellis that is placed in front of it, or the plants can be grown directly over the object. Climbing plants can be aided by attaching a trellis or wires to the wall of the shed or garage, if that is what is being concealed. Some plants are very vigorous and do a good job of hiding what is underneath.

A lick of paint
A simple way to disguise something is to paint it. An oil tank painted green, for example, is more likely to blend into the background than one painted red or white. On the other hand you can make the most of a big surface by decorating it with a mural. This can be something unconnected with the garden, or it can be a vista of some sort, perhaps purporting to be another part of the garden.

Drawing the eye
One way to hide something is to place something else nearby so that the eye goes to that rather than to the eyesore. A pool or a fountain instantly grabs attention, and the nearby shed is likely to be overlooked.

Getting rid of it
A radical solution is to consider whether the eyesore is really needed. A pile of garbage or yard waste can easily be moved and not allowed to reaccumulate. Is the coniper ever likely to be used again? If not, why not dispose of it and rent one when you need it?

Vigorous climbers for hiding eyesores
Clematis montana
Clematis rehderiana
Clematis viticella
Fallopia baldschuanica
Hedera
Humulus
Hydrangea anomala petiolaris
Lonicera periclymenum
Parthenocissus
Rosa
Vitis coignetiae

▶ ▶ Also see: Inner boundaries; pages 120–121

Cover-up
Manhole covers are one of a gardener's nightmares. They are usually unsightly and they cannot be removed or permanently covered up because they have to be accessible. One way of coping with the situation is to cover the manhole with a container of plants. However, do not use too heavy a container, as it may need to be moved.

private space

Staying private

Unless you let the public in on a regular basis, a garden is usually a private space, much in the same way a house is. Unfortunately, unlike a house, the garden is not usually surrounded by solid walls and a roof, and so your privacy may frequently be invaded.

Physical intrusion

Although noise and visual intrusion are often a nuisance, it is the physical intrusion of burglars and others that is the most distressing. A thick, thorny hedge can be a powerful deterrent to burglars as anyone entering must then do so through an entrance that is easier to control. A tall hedge screens a burglar from the public, so for safety, a hedge should not be too tall. Planting spiny plants under windows also acts as a deterrent. Pyracantha is prickly enough to deter most people. Avoid having large bushes near doorways or front paths behind which people can lurk. Discreetly light paths and doorways, possibly using motion-detector lights that switch on as soon someone approaches. The bottom of hedges should be kept dense to keep out unwanted animals (or, indeed, keep them in, if they are your own).

Visual privacy

Most people like their private lives to be private, no matter what it is they are doing. They do not like neighbors or passersby peering into their garden and watching what they are doing. Hedges, fences, and walls are the most effective barriers. Hedges are in many ways the easiest and least expensive option, but they have to be regularly maintained, and the person on the other side of the hedge might not be too keen on cutting his side. He may also not be too happy if your hedge becomes enormous, cutting out sun and light from his garden. A tall fence or trellis with climbers, or a combination of both, is a good alternative. Climbers are not usually as vigorous and contentious as a hedge.

Screens

If it is not possible to put up tall barriers around the garden, it is possible to plant screens within the garden to deflect the view inside. These can also mask activities from neighbors' upstairs windows, which usually have a clear view over fences and hedges. Screens can be localized around an area where people sunbathe or eat, for example. Trees and shrubs may be employed as screens, perhaps playing a dominant part in the garden, or at least around the perimeter of the garden, with a few clear areas for flower beds and entertaining activities left in the middle.

Noise

Unfortunately, the problem of noise intrusion is increasing. Not much can be done about it, although thick, evergreen hedges can help. Entertaining within an inner sanctum such as an arbor or an area surrounded by shrubs helps to reduce the interference.

Smells

Problems with smells and smoke from neighborhood bonfires and barbecues are difficult to tackle. Tall hedges and fences that deflect the flow of air that is carrying the smell or smoke will help, but turbulence inside the boundary will often bring it down again. As it does with windbreaks, a double hedge—one set at a short distance from the other—will help prevent this, but this is usually not a practical method if the garden is small and the nuisance only occasional. Using strongly scented shrubs and perennial plants in the garden can help to counteract smells wafting over the hedge.

Country retreat
Secret hideaways are always worth creating. They allow a place for peace and tranquility in a busy world. In this arbor, the encroaching plants create a womblike retreat where a person can be very private. As well as sitting areas, similar private spaces can be created for sunbathing or eating meals.

outer boundaries

Dividing lines
The easiest form
of outer boundary
to create is a fence.
Like most things in
the garden, there is
no reason why the
gardener should
conform to other
people's ideas.
Create your own
space. A horizontally
boarded fence
(above) has been
decorated with odd
bits of ironwork,
creating an informal
look. The painted
picket-style fence,
(opposite) has a
much more formal
look about it which
fits perfectly with
the clear-cut design
of the garden
and house.

Most gardens come with some form of outer boundary even if it is only a piece of wire stretched between posts. But these can be dissatisfying because they either do not fit in with the design of the garden, or do not really perform their function as a boundary.

Why outer boundaries

There are several reasons why attention should be paid to the outer boundaries of the garden. First, there are the aspects of security and privacy already mentioned in previous pages. But there are also other reasons, more connected with the visual design of the garden. A good hedge, fence, or wall should act as a perfect backdrop to borders or planting within the garden. A dark green hedge, for example, usually sets off the colors of flowers perfectly. They look much more striking than if they have nothing behind them. A fence or wall can be used to house plants or other decorations. Climbing plants, such as roses or clematis, look good in these situations and make a perfect edge to a garden. The wall or fence can also be decorated with window boxes, plaques, water spouts, mosaics, or in a number of other interesting ways. In other words, the boundary is part of the decorative effect of the garden and not just simply something to keep the neighbors out.

What to use

Walls can be beautiful, but they are very expensive, and to be of any value as an outer boundary they must be reasonably high. The choice of color of the brick or stone for a wall is very important. Concrete blocks are an alternative, but far less attractive.

Fences come in all shapes and sizes, from a simple post and rail to solid board. Some are only a token boundary and neither present a barrier against physical or visual intrusion nor are particularly good at supporting plants. Picket fences and wattle hurdles, however, can be very attractive.

Trellising is excellent for supporting plants, but rather see-through and therefore better used for internal boundaries. It can be used effectively to extend the height of fences or walls.

Evergreen hedges make excellent barriers as they are usually impenetrable both physically and visually. Yew is slow-growing but only requires cutting once a year. Leyland cypress roars away but forgets to stop and requires frequent cutting or it is a frequent cause of disputes with neighbors.

Deciduous hedges are generally not as much of a boundary as evergreens, although they are usually just as effective. They are faster-growing than yew and most need at least two trims a year. Most are see-through in winter, although beech and hornbeam generally hold onto their dead leaves.

inner boundaries

Informal hurdles
Country hurdles made from hazel or willow make ideal internal screens. Their rustic quality makes them particularly useful for informal situations, although they can be used in more formal positions where a contrast that is not too extreme is required. However, such hurdles are not a permanent solution as they will deteriorate after a few years.

To many gardeners, the term "inner boundaries" may not seem to make much sense, but here it refers to any form of screen or barrier that is used within the garden. These barriers may be used to screen or delineate different areas of the garden, or simply as a means of supporting climbing plants. A garden broken down into different areas or smaller gardens is always much more interesting than one where everything can be taken in with a single glance. Inner boundaries help to create these partitions. They can also be used for screening eyesores within your own garden.

Trellis

Trellising is a gift for the gardener. It is an ideal barrier between different parts of the garden as it effectively blocks off one part from another, yet allows tantalizing glimpses of what lies beyond. It is ideal for supporting climbers of all types. Trellising helps to create a vertical element that breaks up the garden. Much trellising is attractive in its own right and can be used unadorned. There are many different shapes and patterns of trellising, and it is worth exploring the options before finally deciding what will suit your particular garden design.

Walls

High walls within a small garden can look too solid, making the garden seem even smaller, but low walls definitely have a place, especially for marking off one area of activity from another. The margins of a patio, for example, frequently benefit from having such an edge. Retaining walls are another form of barrier, marking off one level from another.

Hedges

Like walls, tall hedges can be too dominant a feature within a small garden, unless handled carefully; they can form too heavy a barrier. However, tall hedges are ideal for screening off utility areas if you want to prevent garbage bins or compost bins from being seen. Yew is the most attractive material for internal hedges, if you have the patience (a good yew hedge takes five to six years to mature).

Dwarf hedging
Buxus sempervirens 'Suffruticosa'
Lavandula angustifolia
Santolina chamaecyparissus
Teucrium chamaedrys

▶ ▶ Also see: Arches and trellises, pages 104–105; Garden deceits, pages 64–65

Low barriers

Hedges and walls do not have to be tall within a garden. Low box hedges, for example, are excellent for breaking up the garden into compartments or smaller gardens. A fascinating use of dwarf hedges is to create a *parterre* or knot garden, where the hedges are arranged in a decorative pattern, often resembling a knot—the spaces between them are filled with colorful plants. As long as they are not too elaborate these can easily be created in a small garden. A *potager*, or kitchen garden, can be created in a similar way, filling the small beds with vegetables and herbs for the kitchen.

Incidental boundaries

Some forms of boundaries might not be considered as such, but they none-theless form a dividing line between areas. A path, for example, can form a simple boundary between flower borders and vegetable beds. A circle of different-colored bricks on a patio may mark out the space used for a round table, or be used for a particular activity. Visual markers add to the interest of a garden.

Vertical space

Space is often precious in the small garden and every bit of it should be put to use. If internal barriers or screens are required, then the use of trellising allows for the inclusion of climbing plants. This not only allows the gardener to fit in more plants, but makes the garden more three-dimensional. The space becomes more alive.

tool guide

A good set of tools is invaluable to a gardener. The right tool for the job will save a lot of time and effort. However, it is possible to garden successfully with only a few tools. One problem for the small gardener is that the more tools you have, the more space you will need to store them.

Easy storage
Good tools are essential to all gardeners. Only a few are needed for a basic kit, but inevitably a great deal of useful equipment is acquired over the years. A safe, convenient place is required to store them. Painting the handles red so they stand out is a good practice if you are in the habit of losing tools in the flower beds.

Quality
Always buy the best tools you can afford. Cheap tools often bend or corrode very easily. They also lose any sharp edge they have very quickly. Old tools can often be found that are made of excellent quality steel; these are frequently better than their modern equivalents. With modern tools, stainless steel is generally better than ordinary steel, although it is a lot more expensive.

Basic tool kit
Bucket
Gloves
Hand fork
Hoe
Hose
Pitchfork
Pruning saw
Pruning shears
Rake
Spade
Trowel
Watering can

Extra tools
The following tools are desirable but not essential, as most jobs can be performed with the basic tools.

Cultivator
Dibber
Hosepipe
Lawn edgers
Long-arm tree pruners
Loppers
Range of hoes
Sprinklers

Basic equipment
Hedge trimmer
Lawn mower
Wheelbarrow

Extra equipment
The following pieces of equipment are useful, but far from essential. Remember that equipment takes up a lot of storage space and requires maintenance to run properly.

Lawn aerator
Lawn fertilizer spreader
Leaf sweepers
Mechanical cultivator
Shredder

Storage
Tools and equipment should have proper storage; they should not be left lying around in the garden. If there is enough space in a garage then this is ideal. Most tools can be hung from the wall, thus taking up very little space. Equipment, on the other hand, generally takes up floor space. It may be necessary to buy or build a shed to store the tools. This could have a workbench in it for potting and other activities.

Maintenance
Clean all tools and equipment after use. Remove all soil and plant remains, such as leaves and sap and lightly oil the metal surfaces to prevent them rusting. Take particular care at the end of autumn when using things for the last time. All machinery should be maintained and sharpened at least once a year by a professional unless you able to do it yourself.

glossary

aerating Spiking a compacted lawn to allow air to penetrate to the roots.

alpines Theoretically plants from alpine regions, but applies to all plants grown on rock gardens and in alpine houses.

annuals Plants that germinate, flower, seed, and die, all within the one year.

arbor A cavelike structure covered with climbers or made from shrubs. Usually contains seating and sometimes a table.

bare-rooted Plants are thus described if they are dug up from a nursery bed and sold without soil around their roots.

bedding plants Annual and tender perennial plants that are used for mass displays.

biennials Plants that germinate in their first year and flower, seed, and die in their second.

biological control A method of controlling pests by introducing animal predators that eat or live off them.

blind (1) Flowering plants that produce buds that never open.
(2) Covering hardcore or rubble with a layer of builder's sand.

bog garden A border or area of the garden that never dries out and in which moisture-loving plants are grown.

bract A leaf-like appendage that appears just below a flower or forms part of the flower head.

broadcasting A method of sowing seed where the seed is scattered evenly across a surface rather than in rows.

calcareous Alkaline soil containing chalk or lime.

capillary matting A form of matting used in greenhouses that absorbs water from a reservoir and then supplies it to the plants through the bottom of the pots.

catch crop An intermediate crop of vegetables that utilizes temporarily vacant ground.

cascade A stream that runs down a series of waterfalls.

chinoiserie Design in a Chinese style.

clay Heavy, sticky soil that needs to be improved (amended) before it can be used successfully for gardening.

cloche A small, movable frame that is covered in glass or polyethylene and used as a temporary cover for plants, especially vegetables.

climber A plant that climbs through other plants or up walls, fences, and trellises.

clone A plant that has been vegetatively propagated and is identical to its parent.

coir An alternative to peat, made from coconut fiber.

cold frame A miniature greenhouse that serves many of the same functions except that it is low to the ground and thus cannot accommodate the gardener inside of it.

companion planting The use of plants that protect one another from pests and diseases.

compost (1) A special composition of soil used for growing plants in pots and containers. (2) The rotted remains of organic material that is waste from the garden and kitchen.

concrete A mixture of cement and small stones. It is extremely hard and durable.

container Any pot or other vessel for holding plants.

cordon A method of growing low fruit trees that consist basically of a single stem and are usually tied at an angle into wirework.

cottage garden A traditional garden found especially in rural areas, where the design was usually decidedly informal.

crazy paving Paving consisting of broken slabs or stones, arranged randomly.

cultivar A distinct form of a particular species of plant.

cuttings Pieces of stem or root that are put into compost so that they produce roots and eventually become a new plant.

dead-heading Removal of flower heads as they die.

deciduous Plants that lose their leaves during the winter.

decking A constructed wooden surface used as a patio.

division A method of propagating plants by breaking them up into small pieces.

drawn A plant that has become stretched and over-tall due to its search for light.

dry stone wall A stone wall that is built without any mortar or cement.

edging The built-up edge of a lawn or path, laid either to visually or physically contain it.

ericaceous compost Special compost suitable for lime-hating plants, such as rhododendrons and heathers.

espalier A form of training small trees, usually fruiting, against a wall or wires. It generally consists of a main stem with horizontal branches trained along the wires.

evergreen Plants that do not lose their leaves during the winter.

fan A form of training small trees, usually fruiting, against a wall or wires. The branches radiate from a short trunk in the form of a fan.

fasciation A malformation of a plant where the stems or flowers become fused together, giving a straplike appearance. It cannot be transmitted to other plants.

fastigiate A plant that grows like a slender column, upright.

fertilizer A powdered, pelletted or liquid nutrient supplement.

foliage Leaves.

foliar feeding A fertilizer that is applied in liquid form to the leaves of a plant, through which it is absorbed.

fungicide A chemical applied to plants to control fungal diseases.

gazebo A form of open summer house, usually with a view.

germination The development of a seed into a small plant or seedling.

graft The physical union of two plants to form a new one.

gravel Small stones either water worn to size or made by crushing larger stones.

ground cover Plants or any material that covers the ground to suppress weeds and prevent evaporation. **growing bag** Bags filled with compost into which plants can be directly planted.

half-hardy Tender plants (usually annuals) that will not withstand a frost.

hardcore Stones or builders' rubble used as a foundation.

hardening off The process by which seedlings are weaned from a warm indoor atmosphere to an outdoor one ready for planting out.

hardy Capable of withstanding frosts.

herbaceous Strictly speaking, plants that die back to the ground in the winter, but used loosely to refer to any nonwoody perennial plant.

herbicide Chemicals for killing plants, in particular, weeds.

humidity Moisture content of the air.

inflorescence Flower head.

inorganic Material that does not derive from animals or vegetation. Strictly speaking, substances that do not include carbon.

insecticide Chemicals used to kill insects.

kitchen garden Vegetable and herb garden.

knot garden A pattern of low hedges, often filled with colorful bedding or other plants.

lawn An area of grass that is kept relatively short.

leach The process by which nutrients and minerals are washed from the soil by constant rain or watering.

leaf mold Rotted and rotting leaves.

lime Forms of chalk and limestone that are added to the soil to increase its alkalinity.

loam A mixture of clay, sand, and organic material, forming a good, workable soil.

manure Bulky material, usually animal, but can also be plant, used to feed and condition the soil.

maze A series of paths or passages between hedges that form an intricate pattern to the center and exit, which are obscured.

microclimate The local weather pattern.

moisture-retentive soil Soil containing organic material that retains sufficient moisture for plants' needs, but not enough to become waterlogged.

mulch A layer of organic or inert material that is laid over beds to suppress weeds and help preserve moisture.

nursery bed A bed for growing plants until they are big enough to be planted in their final positions.

organic material Material that derives from animal or plant waste.

parterre A series of low hedges forming a pattern, often complicated, the centers of which may be filled with colorful plants.

patio A paved area, often adjacent to the house, mainly used for sitting and entertaining.

pavers Bricks specially made for use in paths, drives, and patios.

perennial (1) Comes up every year. (2) Non-woody plants that continue from one year to the next, although they may die back for the winter.

pergola A series of arches covering a walkway which are often covered with climbing plants.

pesticide A chemical for killing insect pests.

pH The scale against which the acidity/alkalinity of the soil is measured. pH6.6-7.3 is neutral, below is acid, and above is alkaline. Plant growth requires between 5.5 and 7.5; 6.5 is optimum.

potager A vegetable and herb garden, often decorative in its design.

pruning The removal of branches and shoots from plants to improve their shape, health, or performance.

raised beds Beds raised above the surface of the surrounding area, enclosed in low brick, stone, block, or wooden walls.

reversion The return of variegated foliage to its normal green form.

rock plants Theoretically, plants from alpine regions, but applies to all plants grown on rock gardens, and in alpine houses.

rockery A garden or bed built with stone and well-drained soil to provide a natural-looking home for alpine plants.

rotation The process of changing the position of specific crops around the vegetable garden on a three- or four-year basis.

scree A form of very free-draining rock garden consisting mainly of stone that emulates mountain screes.

shrubbery A border devoted entirely to the growth of shrubs.

soak-away A deep hole loosely filled with rubble into which drains bring surface water so that it can slowly soak away rather than remain in the surrounding soil.

soil conditioner Organic material that improves the structure and nutritional value of the soil.

sprinkler A device for automatically spraying water over a large area in the garden.

staging The benching in a greenhouse on which the pots of plants are kept.

staking The supporting of plants using stakes, hoops, or some other device.

standard A form of ornamental or fruit bush that is grown on the top of a single, long stem.

subsoil The soil below the fertile topsoil.

sucker A stem that appears from underground next to a plant.

sunken garden A special part of the of garden that is deliberately sunken below the surrounding area.

terrace (1) A patio. (2) A level piece of ground created on a slope.

tilth The texture of the soil when dug and broken down.

topsoil The fertile top layer of soil.

trellis A wooden screen of crisscrossed slats used to support plants, either freestanding or attached to a wall.

trompe l'oeil A device, usually a painting, that deceives the eye.

trough A stone or cement container for housing a collection of small alpine plants.

underplanting The planting of plants under other, taller ones.

variegated Foliage (but sometimes also flowers) that exhibit more than one color.

vegetative propagation Nonseed methods of propagation using a part of the original plant, such as in taking cuttings or by division.

wattle Pliable stems, usually willow or hazel, woven into panels.

weed killer A chemical used for killing weeds.

wigwam A conical structure of sticks or poles for growing climbing plants.

windbreak Shrubs or netting sited to slow down the wind.

index

acknowledgments

The publishers wish to thank the following organizations for their kind permission to reproduce the photographs in this book:

Clive Nichols Photography *front cover bottom right*, **12** *left*, **13** *bottom left*, **121** *top right*, /designer Richard Coward **4** *top right*, **50-51** *center left*, /designer Dennis Fairweather **52-53** *center right*, /Lisette Pleasance *front cover bottom left*, /Old Rectory, Northants **87** *bottom*, /designer Roger Platts **7** *bottom*, /Vic Shanley **105** *top*, /designer Stephen Woodhams *front cover top left*.

Elizabeth Whiting Associates 23 *top right*, /Andrea V. Einsiedel/designer R. Abel **4** *center left*, **24**, /Michael Dunne **29** *top center*, /A.V. Einsiedel **16**, /Di Lewis **13** *top center left*, /Spike Powell/designers J&N Kent **18-19** *center*.

Garden Picture Library/David Askham **108**, /Lynne Brotchie **4** *center right*, **15** *bottom*, **47** *top right*, /Chris Burrows **70-71** *center left*, /Bob Challinor **120-121** *center*, /David England **44-45** *center right*, **74** *center*, /Ron Evans **79** *top right*, /John Glover *insert p.2 top left, insert p.2 top right*, **41** *top right*, **71** *top right*, **75** *top center*, **112**, /Jaqui Hurst **106-107** *center*, /Roger Hyan **50** *top left*, / Lamontagne **80** *top*, **120** *bottom left*, /Mayer/Le Scanff *insert p.4 top right*, **82**, /Zara McCalmont **56** *top right*, /John Miller **67** *top right*, /John Neubauer **118** *top center*, /Clive Nichols **32** *top right*, **71** *center right*, /Marie O'Hara **28** *top left*, **34-35** *center*, **40-41** *center*, /Jerry Pavia **78** *center left*, **106** *top left*, **107** *top right*, /Howard Rice **10**, **27** *top right*, **39** *top right*, **75** *bottom center*, **98-99** *top center left*, /Gary Rogers **101** *center left*, /John Ferro Sims **4** *bottom left*, **68**, /JS. Sira *insert p.3 topleft*, **36**, **41** *center right*, **44** *top left*, **44** *bottom left*, **48**, **100** *left*, /Freidrich Strauss **21** *left*, /Ron Sutherland **32** *top left*, **92** *top left*, **98** *bottom left*, /Juliette Wade **92** *top right*, /Steven Wooster **18** *bottom left*, **87** *top*.

Garden & Wildlife Matters 22-23 *center*, /Zooid Pictures **34** *top*.

Gardening Which? 86 *top*, **86** *bottom*. John Glover *front cover top right*, **4** *top center*, **13** *center center right*, **13** *top left*, **26-27** *center*, **58** *left*, **78-79** *center right*, **92-93** *center right*, **102**, **104** *right*, /Burford House, Tenbury **96-97** *top center right*, /designer A. Titchmarsh **4** *center*, /designer K. Georgi **84-85** *top center right*, /Great Dixter Garden **58-59** *center*, /Ladywood Hants **116**, /designer P. McCann *back endpaper, front endpaper*, **15** *top*, /designer M. Smith *insert 3 top right*, **38**, /The Dillon Garden **47** *left*, /designer A. Titchmarsh **13** *top right*, **21** *top right*, /designer M. Walker **63** *center*, / designer Geoffrey Whiten **4** *top left*, **54**, /Woking Borough Council **59** *top right*.

Harpur Garden Library Jerry Harpur/designer Robert Chittock, USA **19** *top right*, **97** *bottom center*, /designer Jean M. Clark, Suffolk **9**, /designer Judith Sharpe, London **14** *left*, /designer Barbara Thomas, USA **64-65** *center right*, /designer Bruce Kelly, USA **88**, /designer Christopher Masson, London **62** *top right*, /designer Edwina von Gal, USA **118-119** *center right*, /designer Julie Toll, Herts **114** *left*, /designer Mark Rumary, Yoxford, Suffolk **94**, /designer Michael Balston, Wiltshire **34** *bottom*, /designer Simon Fraser, Teddington, Middx **111**, /designer Vernon Straton **56-57** *center right*, /Dr. Christopher Grey-Wilson, Suffolk **4** *bottom center*, **64** *top center*, /Franchesca Watson, RSA **96** *center left*, /Fuddlers Hall, Essex **66-67** *top center*, /Jenkyn Place, Hampshire **72** *top left*, /Little Malvern Court, Hereford & Worcs. **81** *center*, /Mrs K. Chattaway, Essex **81** *top*, /Oehme & Van Sweden, USA **52** *top left*, /Park Farm, Great Waltham, Essex **90** *top right*, /Sheila Chapman, Essex **110** *right*, /The Priory, Kemerton, Hereford & Worcs **72-73** *center right*, Marcus Harpur/designer Andy Rees, Bucks **100** *right*, /designer Fiona Lawrenson, RHS Chelsea **1997 4** *bottom right*, **60**. Andrew Lawson **3** *center*, **30**, **33** *top center*, **76**, **99** *top right*, **104** *left*, /York Gate, Leeds **23** *center right*.

Harry Smith Collection 22 *left*, **84** *bottom*, **91**, **114-115** *center right*, **122** *right*, **122** *left*, **123**.

Reed Consumer Books Ltd./Andrew Lawson *front cover center left*, **39** *bottom right, insert p.5 center*, /Steve Wooster *back cover center*, **20** *top*, /Polly Wreford *back cover right*, /Neil Holmes **52** *bottom left*, /Jerry Harpur *insert background*.

Robert Harding Picture Library 46 *top right*, **51** *top right*, /Philip Craven **42**, /Family Circle/photographer Debbie Patterson *back cover left*, /Homes & Gardens IPC Magazines LTD/Polly Wreford *insert p.4 top left*, **28** *top right*, /Simon Upton **7** *top*.